Reflections on Our Holy Holidays

Lloyd Elias Scalyer

Lititz Institute
Publishing Division

© 2018 by Lloyd Elias Scalyer (author)

For further Information please write to the author:

The National Center and MHCF
PO Box 92
Ronks, PA 17572

Published by Lititz Institute Publishing Division

PO Box 3310
Sequim, WA 98382
www.lititzinstitute.org

All rights reserved. Written permission must be secured from the author to use or reproduce any part of this book, except for brief quotations.

Printed in the United States of America

Library of Congress Cataloguing-in-Publication Data

Scalyer, Lloyd Elias
Reflections on Our Holy Holidays/ Lloyd Elias Scalyer

cm.

ISBN 978-1-7322869-0-0   (paperback)

The Holy Holidays: 1. How and when they were established. 2. How they were celebrated. 3. What the implications of these holidays are under the New Covenant.

ACKNOWLEDGEMENTS

It is with great humility that I thank the L-rd G-d Almighty for His wonderful guidance in writing this book. Without His guidance and input I never would have been able to complete these messages and hence this book. He is majestically majestic and marvelously marvelous and does all things according to the counsel of His own will (Eph. 1:11). May He truly be continually glorified through His word.

To my beloved wife Judith, who is the love of my life. I first saw her walking in the front of my house in Brooklyn New York on June 25, 1960, and we were married on August 28. She is a tremendous inspiration to me, and I owe her more than I can possibly say. She encouraged me to complete the book, based on my messages at the Seed of Abraham and has put up with my taking time to complete this project.

I would also like to thank Dr. Alta Ada Williams, who gave me immeasurable help and guidance with my Hebrew and Greek, and Dr. Bruce Williams, who helped with the layout of everything before the manuscript was finalized and the book printed.

Members of the Seed of Abraham Messianic Congregation were a great encouragement to me as I worked on this book—especially Sara Linton, Maria Riley, Rosetta Stauffer, Dr. Joseph Wehrer, Dr. John Metzger, Professor Rob Perlis, Dr. Maria Perlis, Pam Hjelm, and Kimmel and Stephanie Schaefer.

Table Of Contents

Foreword	8
Introduction	9
Prolgue	27
Passover	39
Unleavened Bread	71
The Feast of Weeks	83
The Feast of Trumpets	97
Yom Kippur	117
The Feast of Tabernacles	137
Shemini Atzeret	153
The Sabbath	165

Foreword

This book is a compilation of messages on the Levitical feasts of the Lord brought by the author to The Seed of Abraham, a Messianic fellowship in Lititz Pennsylvania. I discuss the reasons behind the compiling of the book in the Introduction.

Since the various chapters are, in general, individual messages that were delivered to that group, I have left the sometimes colloquial speech and the direct address to the audience intact. More formal presentations would be more impersonal, and it is my wish that the reader will receive from the messages what was intended for the original recipients.

Several notes need to be made. All Scripture quoted, unless otherwise noted, is from *The Holy Bible, New International Version®*, Copyright © 1973, 1978, 1984 by International Bible Society. Used by permission of Zondervan Publishing House. Other Versions and their abbreviations are: The Authorized King James Version of the Holy Bible (KJV), The New King James Version (NKJV), and the New American Standard Version (NAS). When a word does not appear in the original language but is supplied by the translator, that word is put in italics. I have left those italics as in the translation. When I add italics for emphasis, I note this by stating, "Emphasis added."

Two explanations are necessary concerning grammatical points. In Standard English, pronouns must agree in number and gender with their antecedents. Whenever the gender could be either male or female and when the work is singular and since the gender is not specified, the masculine is used. Modern "politically correct" writers frequently avoid this situation by making the pronoun plural: "Each believer must decide for himself what he will do." Since believer is singular and since the gender is not specified the masculine is used. Modern "politically correct: writers frequently avoid this situation by making the pronoun plural: "Each believer must decide for themselves what they will do." Alternately, some writers use the awkward "Each believer must decide for himself what he or she will do." Neither of these attempts to avoid using the masculine pronoun is acceptable, the former one being incorrect grammar and the latter being very awkward. Thus, in this book we have used the traditional English concerning a believer or an individual. It should be understood to apply equally to males and females except where context specially precludes this reading. In addition, normal usage refers to a country as feminine. ("The United States is a country in which her people have come from many nation.") Therefore, when we speak Israel, we use the feminine singular to refer to her and to her people.

My prayer is always that Jeh-vah El-him receive all the glory. It is with this wish that I submit this treatise.

Introduction

The Occasion for and Purpose of the Book

Yeshua-Jesus the Messiah is the subject of all of Scripture that which was written before His advent as well that which came after. He made this claim Himself in Luke 24:27, 44-47 and in John 5:46, where He told the Jewish leaders, "If you believed Moses, you would believe me, for he wrote about me." This book will examine the Levitical feasts, the effect G-d intended them to have on Israel, and the way in which they point to the great work G-d would do through Messiah Yeshua. Our prayer is that a better understanding of these feasts will increase your appreciation for G-d's glorious provision of salvation through His Son and enable you to use the Older Testament Scriptures to reveal Messiah to those of natural Israel that G-d is pleased to bring into your lives.

In the fall of 1983 I was discussing the Levitical feasts with a dear friend of mine. I told him that I thought the Levitical feasts had been fulfilled Biblically or else the New Covenant could not be in effect at this time. We discussed this for a while, and then he suggested that I write a book stating the facts as I saw them. I told him that I would give him the facts and that he should write the book. He said to me, "Not a chance Lloyd; if you want the Biblical facts to come out, you will have to write the book."

I was really not interested in writing a book of any kind whatsoever. I have been of the opinion for many years now that it is too easy for believers to have a great thirst for learning but not nearly as great a thirst for applying those lessons toward holiness in their lives. The last thing that is needed is another book. A couple of years later my wife also suggested to me that I should take what was in my head and put it down on paper in the form of a book on the Levitical feasts. But it was to no avail; I still did not see a need for the book to be written.

Over the years the Holy Spirit has laid two great burdens on my shoulders. They are the salvation of the Jewish people and the fact that I believe that most believers will not do well when they explain before the throne of Messiah the things that they have done while living on this earth. The Holy Spirit showed me that if I wrote a book explaining the Levitical feasts, I would help alleviate both burdens.

While the burden for the salvation of the Jewish people is obvious, the burden for born-again believers is not. The apostle to the Gentiles tells us in Romans 11:11: "Again I ask: Did they stumble so is to fall beyond recovery? Not at all! Rather, because of their transgression, salvation has come to the Gentiles to make Israel envious." (Emphasis added)

A few years ago I was at a conference in Lexington, Kentucky. After speaking to the conference for a few minutes, I recounted Romans 11:11 and asked those in attendance if there were any one of them who had made a Jewish person envious of his love for the Jewish Messiah. Out of fourteen hundred people there were only two people who could give a positive response. When I am in other similar situations, I often ask the same question; and invariably not one person can respond positively. It is my experience that out of the great number of believers, there are only a small number who do try to reach the Jewish people for Messiah and to make them envious of their love for him. Many people tell me of their love for the Jewish people. When they do, I ask them a series of questions:

Do you pray for the peace of Jerusalem? A few will answer "Yes."

Do you pray for the salvation of the Jewish people? Some answer that they do while most say that they do not.

Do you support a mission to the Jews with prayer and/or finances? Invariably the answer is "No."

Do you support an individual Jewish missionary with prayer and/or finances? Invariably the answer is "No."

These are the answers that I receive from the vast majority of believers. They are not the answers that I receive from some few members of varied churches or all members of Messianic congregations. Their answers to the above questions would be absolutely in the affirmative rather than the negative.

Imagine this scenario: the L-rd Messiah speaks to believers and says to them, "The apostle to the Gentiles told you clearly that I broke off some of the natural branches so that I could graft you in to make Israel envious. He warned you not to boast against the natural branches, and you have done so both in your theology and in your actions. I wept over Jerusalem. Why didn't you?" What will they say when our L-rd says, "I longed to gather the Jewish people as a mother hen gathers her chicks but they would not? Why didn't you long to gather them as I longed to gather them? I cried as I broke off those branches and rejoiced as I grafted you in. Why couldn't you rejoice in your salvation and seek to share it with them? They are bone of my bone and flesh of my flesh." Most believers that I know would not do well under this kind of questioning from our L-rd. It is my fervent desire that they would instead hear the words, "Well done thou good and faithful servant." I fear that they will not hear those words with regard to this matter, because their hearts and their minds have chosen not to follow the L-rd in the matter of making Israel envious.

In Genesis 9:27 Noah makes this very telling statement: "'May God extend the territory of Japheth; may Japheth live in the tents of Shem, and may Canaan be his slave.'" Evangelicalism today tells us that the first part of that statement has been completed because the descendants of Japheth (the Indo-Europeans) have come to the God of Shem. The fact is that there are a small portion of believers who live in the tents of Shem, while the rest do not. For the most part, the descendants of Japheth have not entered into the tents of Shem. In reality, they have received salvation from the G-d of Shem but they have not entered into the tents of the descendants of Shem. When a person enters into someone's tent or home, he becomes part and parcel of his existence. As a general rule, the great majority of believers have not done this, nor are they interested in doing this. It is by not sharing the gospel with Israel that they are boasting against the natural branches (Rom. 11:17ff).

Every believer who has received salvation since the time that Messiah was crucified has been saved under the New Covenant (Jer.

31:31ff.). This covenant tells us in verse 36 that the descendants of Israel are a nation before Almighty G-d. As G-d defines the existence of Israel, each individual Jewish person, regardless of where he may live, is considered to be part of the nation of Israel. When someone goes to an individual Jewish person, he is going to the nation. Israel, according to El-him, is the only nation that He has spread over the face of the earth. She is everywhere that believers are, and believers have a special responsibility toward her, wherever the individuals are found. In Matthew 28:19 Messiah tells us to make disciples of all nations, baptizing them in the name of the Father and the Son and the Holy Spirit. Since Israel is a nation, believers are required to bring the gospel to her also.

When we send a missionary to a foreign field, we make sure that he learns the culture as well as the language. He must know the customs as well as the mindset of the people he is going to serve in the name of Messiah. When it comes to Jewish missions, very few believers learn the mindset of the Jewish people. They assume that the Jewish people regard the concepts of salvation, heaven, hell, sacrifice, and atonement in the same way that they do, with minor variations. This of course is a big fallacy.

It is my hope that the L-rd Almighty will use this book to show believers how to make Israel envious, as well as to prick the hearts of believers in their association with the Jewish people, so that they may hear the words, "Well done thou good and faithful servant." It is also my hope that it will be used in witnessing to Jewish people so that they may learn of the great love of Messiah Yeshua (Jesus). To that end, I will use the Hebrew names for Jesus, L-rd, and G-d.

Many people talk about G-d without knowing anything about Him. They come up with all kinds of fanciful ideas about Him without seeking the reality of the Holy Scriptures which are His self revelation.

El-him is the only word used for G-d in the first chapter of Genesis. It is a plural noun that is used more than twenty-five hundred times in the Older Covenant Scriptures. The singular form, El-ha is rarely used. At times in the Scripture this plural noun El-him is combined with singular verbs or adjectives. This combination shows that the singular Godhead is comprised of more than one. I love the example in Psalms 77:13b, "Who is so great a G-d (El [singular]) as our G-d (El-him [plural])?"

Numbers 6:24-26, Isaiah 54:5, and Isaiah 48:16ff. are some examples from the Older Covenant Scripture intimating that the Godhead might be comprised of three entities (but definitely more than one entity), all acting as one. The doxology of Israel in Deuteronomy 6:4 is another good example. It says, "Hear, O Israel: YH-H our El-him YH-H is one. The L-RD our G-d, the L-RD is one." The one is echad which is a compound unity noun meaning "one comprised of more than one."

YH-H meaning L-rd, is another name of El-him and is used over sixty-eight hundred times in the Older Covenant Scriptures. It is usually used when G-d's covenantal relationship is emphasized. This word is introduced in the second chapter of Genesis. In Genesis 2:4 the wordsL-rd G-d in most English translations are YH-H El-him. Jeh-vah is self existent from everlasting to everlasting; therefore He could say to Moses, "I am that I am." In the second and third chapters of Genesis, wherever YH-H is mentioned, El-him is always added. The only exceptions are when the woman and the serpent speak. The Older Covenant Scriptures show Jeh-vah to be personal to G-d's individually; that is why He reveals so many attributes in conjunction with His name.

Jeh-vah El-him: The L-rd G-d. Genesis 2:4.

Jeh-vah Elyon: The L-rd most high. Genesis 14:18-20.

Jeh-vah Rapha: The L-rd our healer. Exodus 15:26.

Jeh-vah Nissi: The L-rd my banner. Exodus 17:15.

Jeh-vah Shalom: The L-rd our peace. Judges 6:24.

Jeh-vah Tsidkenu: The L-rd our righteousness. Jeremiah 23:6.

About the third century B.C. the rabbis became reluctant to use the name YH-H, so they used the name Ad-nai instead. Ad-nai is an emphatic form of adon which means "l-rd" or "master." Ad-nai is used of earthly masters, as when Sarah called Abraham "L-rd" it is this servant relationship that is emphasized when Ad-nai is applied to G-d. The person using this word is in a definite personal relationship to Ad-nai. He is in the subordinate position of being a servant or slave to his master. In Genesis 24:9, 10, 12, 14, 27, 35 and Exodus 21:4-6 the term is also used to describe a wife who is subject to her husband.

I learned vividly the concept of subordination while I was in Headquarters Company 71st Regiment 42nd Division, as a "guest" of our Uncle Sam. The first lesson I learned was that I was no longer my own. I was the property of the United States government, period. My opinions and my thoughts were of no great importance to anyone but me. I did what I was told, or I paid the consequences. I was told very clearly and plainly, "Yours is not to reason why, yours is but to do and die." The second precept I learned was that I must salute each officer regardless of whether I thought he deserved the salute. In saluting, I was actually saluting the uniform and not the officer.

These two lessons worked very well for me in my experience as a believer. I realized that I was bought with a price and I was no longer my own. That price was the sacrifice of Yeshua- Jesus the Messiah. As a believer, I am His and He is mine. He makes the decisions as to what I am to do; and it is my duty to accomplish His bidding in my life for His glory. While it is true that as a believer I am not required to do great things in His name, I am required to be faithful to try to accomplish all He gives me to do. Isaiah 55:8, 9 tells us: "For my thoughts are not your thoughts, neither are your ways my ways…as the heavens are higher than the earth, so are my ways higher than your ways and my thoughts than your thoughts."

It is not for me to understand why Yeshua said through the apostle Paul in Romans 1:16 that the gospel is to go to the Jew first. It is also not for me to understand why our L-rd said in Romans 2:9 that tribulation will come to the Jew first, even though all have sinned and come short of the glory of G-d (Rom. 3:23). Romans 10:12 tells us that there is no difference between Jew and Gentile-the same L-rd is L-rd of all, and richly blesses all who call on Him, for everyone who calls on the name of the L-rd will be saved. Nevertheless, after all of this has been said, the fact still remains that the L-rd of glory, Yeshua- Jesus the righteous, says that the Gentiles are to make the Jewish people envious. It is my intention in this book to show my brethren, the Jewish people, the way to salvation that has been provided by The L-rd our G-d. I also intend to show Gentile believers how they can accomplish the feat of making Israel envious of their love for the Jewish Messiah. In doing so they will be giving the L-rd Messiah all the glory, while reserving none for themselves. Yeshua is the Hebrew name of Jesus. It means salvation, and it is free for the asking.

Introduction 15

Overview of the Levitical Feasts

The Book of Leviticus gives us a list of the great feasts of the Jewish religion. There were a total of nine feasts:

The L-rd's Passover (vs. 3-5)

The Feast of Unleavened Bread (vs.6-8)

The Feast of Firstfruits (vs 9-14)

The Feast of Weeks (vs. 15-22)

The Feast of Trumpets (vs. 23-25)

The Day of Atonement (vs. 26-32)

The Feast of Tabernacles (vs. 33-43)

Shemini Atzeret [the eighth assembly (vs. 36)]

The Weekly Sabbath (vs. 3)

We will discuss 1-7 as the seven Levitical feasts, then Shemini Atzeret, the eighth assembly. Following these we will treat the weekly and special Sabbaths.

All Evangelicals agree that the feasts are types or pictures of our L-rd Yeshua- Jesus, the Messiah of Israel, and His redemptive work. However, the particular prophetic view one holds will have some effect on the understanding of just how each feast pictures Messiah and His work.

The very life and worship of the nation of Israel was built around these feasts. The Levitical feasts were given to the Israelites as a sign that the daily affairs of their lives were secondary to their fellowship with their L-rd. To help them strive for holiness, they were to spend these specific times with their Creator and Sustainer. The feasts were actually convocations, which meant that the people were summoned to observe them regularly. The observances of all the feasts were designed by G-d to take Israel's eyes off earthly things and put them on heavenly things.

The feasts were a precursor to the time when El-him's (G-d's) true redeemed children would worship Him in "spirit and truth." When the fulfillment of the truth set forth in these feasts was accomplished, G-d's people would enjoy the fullness of the Spirit. There would be a time in the future when their fellowship would not be restricted to mere stated periods of time, but it would be for all times and in all areas of life. They would begin a completely new life that would finally consummate in heaven itself.

This lesson of coming apart from their daily activities was applicable for the regular seventh-day Sabbaths, as well as the feast days and special Sabbaths. In that age the Spirit of the Almighty One was not permanently and personally resident in the heart of true believers in the sense that He has been since Pentecost. The L-rd, therefore set aside Sabbaths when the people would separate themselves from that which marked their earthly existence and seek YH-H and His paths of righteousness. It must be remembered that every feast day was a Sabbath regardless of what day of the week it occurred, and every Sabbath carried identical conditions and characteristics. Physical work was punished by death on each of the feast days just as it was on the seventh-day Sabbath.

You might ask why it is so important to learn about the convocations of Israel. "How can such a study help me in my walk with G-d, today?" The answer is quite simple: the feasts of Leviticus 23 link the Older and the Newer Covenants. All that has been given in picture form, or type, is fulfilled in Yeshua (Jesus) the Messiah. To understand the feasts is to understand His great work of redemption. An equally good reason to understand the meaning of the feasts, or convocations, is that this will greatly help anyone to explain El-him's plan of redemption to a non-believing Jewish person.

The sacrifices and offerings were an important part of all the feasts. It is primarily in the feasts and offerings that the gospel is preached in the Older Covenant (Testament) Scriptures. The concept of making sacrifice to El-him (G-d, plural) did not begin with the instructions given to Moses any more than salvation by faith through grace began with the advent of Messiah. There are instances in the Scripture where individuals who were "saved by faith" sacrificed to El-him long before the law was ever given to Moses on Mount Sinai, Abel (Gen. 4:4), Noah (Gen. 8:20), Abraham (Gen.15:9 ff.; 21:2-13), Jacob (Gen. 31:54; 35:1-15), Job (Job 1:5). Presumably El-him initiated blood sacrifice as that which is acceptable to Him in the Garden of Eden after the fall (Gen. 3:21). The difference was that the sacrifices required during the Levitical feasts had a separate and distinct purpose.

Israel was promised that if she fulfilled El-him's covenant law, she would become a holy nation and a kingdom of priests. She never achieved that status. Even though the Almighty One had provided a system of forgiveness for the Israelites, they repeatedly forsook El-him's ways for their own ways. Jeh-vah had created them out of the Gentiles to do His will, not their own, just as He has created believers to do His will and not their own. As history unfolds, we see that Israel was much like her Gentile predecessors; she did not seek El-him's ways but instead followed the imaginations of her own heart. Since the fall of mankind, related in Genesis 3, it has been the natural inclination of mankind to focus on earthly things as opposed to spiritual things. Israel's rebellion was more grievous than that of the Gentiles, because G-d had given her so much truth in revelation. Now, in this Church age, under the New Covenant, the rebellion of all mankind (both Jew and Gentile) against Messiah Yeshua-Jesus is the epitome of being hard-hearted and having a stiff neck. Natural Israel looked through a glass darkly, while those in this age have seen the full light and revelation of Messiah, even though they may not have understood it.

Not only during the feasts, but also during their daily lives, Israelites where to separate themselves from earthly trials and tribulations and to focus upon the monotheistic triune G-dhead. In the times since the destruction of the Temple in A.D.70, Israel has focused on El-him as being singularly monotheistic, a single entity by Himself. The Jewish Scriptures teach differently. They teach that El-him (G-d) is plural. In fact, El-him is used more than twenty-five hundred times in the Older Covenant Scriptures. The feasts are actually completed not only by the work of the L-rd Yeshua the Messiah, but also by the work of the total G-dhead in unison.

When Israelites celebrate the feasts, they do so in the legalistic, natural sense and not in the spiritual sense. They are blinded to the reality of the G-dhead and therefore cannot celebrate the feasts in spirit and in truth. To understand the feasts, one must understand the G-dhead; and natural Israel, comprised of those who still reject her Messiah, does not understand real spiritual truth. She recites her own doxology, yet is blinded to its meaning. She knows the words, but not the Maker of the words.

Israel's doxology is found in Deuteronomy 6:4: "Hear, O Israel: the L-RD our G-d, the L-RD is one (Shema Yisrael Ad-nai El-hanu Ad-nai Echad)." YH-H is plural, meaning "l-rds." El-hanu is plural and Echad is a compound unity noun meaning "one comprised of more than one." The doxology literally means, "The L-rd, our G-ds, the L-rds is one." Here there was one G-dhead, as opposed to the many gods of the heathen. That one G-dhead is not a single entity comprised of only one distinct person, but that G-dhead entity is in reality comprised of more than one person.

If the Almighty One were actually one and only one in the single sense, then the doxology would end with Yachid showing one singular instead of Echad showing one comprised of more than one. But that is not the Hebrew rendition of Deuteronomy 6:4. The rendition shows that there is a multiplicity in the one G-dhead. All the persons operate, think, and work as one. This would definitely be in contradistinction to the gods of the Gentiles who were separate individuals, very often did their own things, and were sometimes at cross-purposes with each other.

The feasts pointed to the great salvation that the L-rd was providing. The L-rd always had His own redeemed people from the beginning of time, and He will continue to have His own redeemed people until the end of time. From before the foundations of the earth, the Master Potter knew each and every vessel that would be given His spirit and each and every vessel that would not be given His spirit.

With the unfolding of each book of the Holy Scriptures we see clearly that His ways are higher than our ways, and that we can we can never fully understand His ways. Salvation was always through faith by the grace of G-d. Blood was always needed for the remission of sin. Ad-nai (in the triune aspect) set that blood aside to pay for the sin of all those who were to be redeemed. Messiah was the one who was sent to earth to shed that blood. Calvary was the real Day of Atonement. There was no actual atonement prior to when Messiah fully paid the penalty of sin by His death. The word atonement means "covering". The animal's blood that was shed on the Day of Atonement was like an I.O.U. that had to wait for Messiah's sacrifice before sin could be paid for. Before Messiah came, sins were 'covered' by the blood of animal sacrifices, but they were not actually paid for until Messiah died under the curse of G-d on the Cross.

All Scripture, from Genesis to Revelation, shows us that fallen man has a mind that will lead him to do his own will rather than the will of El-him. Mankind does not have the ability to raise itself from the natural realm to the spiritual realm. Only the spirit of the Triune El-him, visiting fallen man, can raise that fallen person to sit in the heavenlies.

To the Jewish mind, and for that matter to anyone with a rational historical mindset, the G-d of the Jews and the G-d of the Christians could not be the same person. People calling themselves Christians have committed all manner of filthy debauchery upon the Jewish people in the name of the One they said was the Jewish Messiah. This is the same Jewish Messiah who wept over the Jewish people and longed to gather them as a mother hen gathers her chicks. Jews know that Christians say that their G-d is love and mercy, but the fact is that people who have called themselves Christians have killed and maimed the Jewish people with the sword for two thousand years. Some evangelical Christians have been friends to the Jewish people, while others have treated then within indifference or contempt.

As a general rule it is impossible for a murderer to get into the kingdom of heaven (Romans 21:8). Those who have persecuted and murdered the Jewish people for the past two thousand years were children of their father the devil. However, we know that El-him is sovereign in all things and that it is possible that someone who was a persecutor and murderer could have repented of his sin (2 John 2:2). Scripture itself indeed records just such a case with respect to the Apostle Paul. We do not assume, however, that those who commit murder in Messiah's name and never repent are truly His followers.

I have a question for each reader. Is your attitude toward the Jewish people a valid reflection of the Savior's attitude toward them? Do you weep for the lost people of the house of Israel in the same manner as the greatest sin-bearer who ever came into this world wept? Do you weep as your Savior and L-rd wept?

He broke off some of his earthly brethren who were the natural branches so that you, who are a wild olive branch, could be grafted into His tree and receive everlasting life with Him (Romans 11:17-24). He weeps as He breaks off His own and grafts you in. Even though Israel looked through a glass darkly, G-d punished her because she did not practice mercy. True believers who have seen the light have a greater responsibility than Israel ever had to show mercy. May we never marvel that Israel was guilty of withholding mercy, when we know that if it were not for the grace of G-d, we would be just as hard-hearted as she was. I wonder what excuse born-again believers who do not show mercy to Israel will give when they stand before the one and only Messiah.

Those of us who live after the time of Messiah's sacrifice have no excuse. We are given the command to love our neighbor as ourselves. We are also told to be merciful, just as our Father is merciful. As Adnai freely showed mercy to true believers, so true believers are to show mercy to others.

El-him speaks to us regarding the ingrafted branches in Romans 11:11. Salvation has come to the Gentiles to make Israel envious. If Israel is not jealous, it may be that Gentiles who believe in Messiah Yeshua- Jesus have failed to do their part in giving El-him glory in this matter.

The L-rd G-d tells Israel through Isaiah that He will restore her. He says He will never forget her and that she is engraved on the palms of His hands. He tells Israel that He will beckon to the Gentiles and that He will lift up His banner to the peoples. He says that the Gentiles will bring Israel's sons in their arms and carry their daughters on their shoulders (Isa. 49:16 & 22ff). This great promise to Israel should be an encouragement to born again believers to reach out to the Jewish community both corporately and individually.

When talking to knowledgeable Orthodox Jewish theologians about Yeshua, the answer we hear is that Yeshua is a non-entity. He is someone who, even if He did exist at one time, is of no importance. Is it possible that if, historically, Jewish people had been shown love and compassion by those who call themselves followers of the Jewish Messiah Yeshua, they might have gained some recognition of the significance He makes in the lives of those He touches? Now, when some Christians would seek to show them love, the standard Jewish answer is, "You couldn't kill us; now you want to convert us." Strange and disheartening as it may seem, all of this is under the sovereignty of Almighty G-d. The Jewish people will see and understand the significance of Yeshua in G-d's good time and to His own great glory. Even though G-d is sovereign in this matter, believers are not excused from fulfilling the responsibility G-d has given them to make Israel envious.

Followers of Judaism not only have not been made envious, they fail to understand the need for a substitutionary blood atonement. Consider the example of Amnon of Mainz who lived in the twelfth-century AD and was martyred for his Jewish faith.1 The Archbishop of Mainz urged Amnon to renounce Judaism and be baptized. Amnon continually refused. The Archbishop became exasperated and ordered that Amnon's hands and feet be mutilated. As he lay dying from his wounds, he composed this prayer that is recited in the Synagogue on the evening service before the day of Rosh Hashanah (the Feast of Trumpets) and on Yom Kippur (The Day of Atonement).

We will celebrate the mighty holiness of this day, for it is one of awe and terror. Thereon your dominion is exalted and your throne is established in mercy, and you sit thereon in truth. It is you alone who are the judge and the arbiter, who knows and are witness; you write down and set the seal, you record and you tell; you remember the things that have been forgotten. You unfold the records, and the deeds that are inscribed within proclaim themselves; for the seal of every man's hand is set thereto. The great trumpet is sounded; the still small voices heard; the angels are dismayed; fear and trembling seize hold of them as they proclaim, Behold the Day of Judgment! The host of Heaven is to be arraigned in judgment. For in your eyes they are not pure; and all who enter the world you cause to pass before yourself as a flock of sheep. As a shepherd seeks out his flock, and causes them to pass beneath His crook, so do you cause to pass and number, tell and visit appointing the measure of every creature's life and decreeing their destiny.

(Found in smaller various versions of Synagogue prayer books for Rosh Hashanah and Yom Kippur holidays.)

The underlying belief of this prayer is that atonement and forgiveness depend on whether a man's good deeds and merits outweigh his misdeeds and demerits. The basic weakness of Judaism is that it is aware of sins, but in fact ignores "sin". It ignores the essential bias of man toward evil. It ignores man's total depravity and the sinfulness of his nature. Rabbinic Judaism has totally misrepresented the L-rd G-ds means of salvation. It divides sin into different classes with different forms of repentance for each class. Since there is no longer an operating priesthood, the interpretation of the Scriptures is left to the rabbis who rely on the oral law as codified in the Talmud to decide issues of importance. In effect, they say that the Day of Atonement offers atonement without the necessity of an animal blood sacrifice. They maintain that effectual atonement for sin is accomplished by an individual's good works.

Rabbinic Judaism has misunderstood the nature of the salvation to which the feasts pointed. In reality, the feasts had two functions. The first was to draw Israel away from the world and cause her to look to Jehovah. The second was to give her a picture of what would happen when the feasts were fulfilled. Adonai was leading Israel from the natural to the spiritual, even though the entire nation did not "make the trip." There would be a period in time when the Older Covenant would be fulfilled and the Jewish New Covenant promised in Jeremiah 31:31ff would be enacted.

With the coming of Messiah and the inauguration of the New Covenant, of the Levitical feasts have been fulfilled; two of them however, still have some further fulfillment to come. If these convocations were not fulfilled in Yeshua the Messiah, then their ritual legalistic observance would still be a pathway for man to commune with G-d. This cannot be, since Yeshua said, "None can come to the Father but by me" (John 6:44). The fact that Messiah completed these convocations is very telling. We will see that the convocations always pointed to a redemption that was going to be provided for mankind. Messiah is the only pathway to our Father in heaven. Each of the convocations does its particular part in glorifying Yeshua the Son. During the last convocation in this series, the feast of Shemini Atzeret, we will see clearly that all things are completed in Messiah. When this completion was accomplished, all those who were born again (and those who would be born again) by the spirit of El-him were, are and will be able to sit in heavenly places with Him (Ephesians 2).

All of the animal sacrifices in one way or another prefigured the perfect sacrifice of Messiah Yeshua. He is the only sacrifice that Almighty G-d would accept for the redemption of all those people who would come to Messiah in faith. Our heavenly Father not only made the New Covenant for man's salvation, but He also provided the only sacrifice that He would accept to pay for man's sin.

Messianic believers celebrate all the feasts in light of their completion because of Messiah's sacrifice. We do not celebrate them under the law, which had dominion over the people who lived and worshipped under the Older Covenant. Rather, we celebrate the feasts in their fulfillment in the sacrifice of Messiah Yeshua. Since the time of the destruction of the Temple by Rome, rabbinic Judaism has taught and strongly maintained that all men have an absolute free will. It stoutly maintains that, with this free will, man is able to do works of righteousness that will cause him to inherit eternal life in the celestial kingdom. It also maintains that mankind was not conceived in sin and that a new baby is sinless. Further, it also maintains that the Jewish people are the suffering servant mentioned in Isaiah 53.

According to this system, since the Jewish people are the suffering servant very little righteousness is needed on their part for them to enter the eternal kingdom. In fact, not only do the rabbis think that Israel is the suffering servant, bet they also think that Israel suffers for the sins of the Gentiles. Some parts of the Jewish community strictly celebrate the Levitical feasts (except for the sacrifices), while other parts of the Jewish community do not celebrate the feasts at all.

I would be remiss if I did not mention that the L-rd Messiah said, "You must be born again." He said that this new birth was to be a birth of spirit and water (John 3:5). The natural birth is in the natural realm, and the spiritual birth is in the heavenly realm. Unregenerate man can never raise himself from the natural birth to the spiritual birth. The spiritual birth is a sovereign act of El-him's free grace. He chooses those upon whom He will set that grace.

The Lord's Supper and these feasts are the only holiday celebrations authorized in the Scriptures. Both the Lord's Supper and the feasts constantly point us to the Author and Finisher of our faith. We celebrate them in the Spirit. To celebrate them under the authority of the Older Covenant administration would negate the authority and finality of the New Covenant. If New Covenant believers would celebrate the Levitical feasts in spirit and in truth, giving glory to the Messiah of Israel who fulfilled the feasts, they would cause Israel to become envious and fulfill Romans 11:11. Since Messiah is the Word who was made flesh, He is the embodiment of all the law, the prophets, and the writings. He is the only one who could close the Older Covenant as well as open the new one. He is the supreme lawgiver and is the only one who has the right to change the law. In changing the law, He does not make a new way of salvation, for man has always been saved by grace through faith. Under the New Covenant, G-d's people are held to an even higher standard of behavior than they were under the older one, because G-d's moral character has been more completely revealed. It is in the light of this fuller revelation that we may celebrate the feasts without returning to the Older Covenant.

As we celebrate the feasts in spirit and in truth, we thereby testify to the children of Israel the validity and superiority of the teachings of Messiah over the teachings of Moses. Again, we are to understand that Messiah is the Word who was made flesh to come and dwell among us. He, being the Word, gave the word to Moses to give to the nation of Israel. He is the supreme lawgiver. To Messiah Yeshua belongs all honor and glory both now and forever more. He is our Sabbath rest in addition to being the one who upholds us and sustains us all the days of our life.

The overview of the feasts in the fulfilled biblical sense is as follows:

Passover reminds us of the sacrifice of Messiah.

Unleavened Bread reminds us of His sinlessness and His time in the lower parts of the earth.

Firstfruits reminds us of His resurrection and that He is the firstfruits of the new creation.

The Feast of Weeks reminds us of the initiation and ratification of the New Covenant.

The Feast of Trumpets announces to us that atonement has been accomplished by Messiah. It will also be blown to announce the heavenly wedding of Messiah and His bride.

The Day of Atonement authenticates the sacrifice of G-d's lamb.

The Feast of Tabernacles is fulfilled when a person is regenerated and the

Spirit of the living G-d indwells him. It will be completely fulfilled when all believers of all time will dwell with Yeshua in spirit and in truth in His everlasting Kingdom.

Shemini Atzeret verifies as fact that in the end of all sacrificing, only one sacrifice (the sacrifice of Yeshua) was needed to pay for all sin.

The Sabbath proclaims that Yeshua is our Sabbath rest.

As we study and discuss these festivals, it behooves every one of us to keep our eyes on the Cross and upon the sacrifice of our L-rd and Savior. The L-rd shall reign forever and ever. There will be a day coming when the L-rd and His people will dwell as one in the heavenly Kingdom that has been prepared for them from before the foundations of this earth were laid.

All glory in our lives belongs to the L-rd G-d Almighty.

Prologue

The Grace of our Father our King to a Natural Branch

Note: Throughout this book on the Levitical Feasts, the author has included many testimonies to the grace of our heavenly Father in the lives of Jewish people. The following is the author's testimony to our Father's work of grace in his own life.

I never thought in my wildest dreams that I would ever become a follower of Jesus the Messiah. How could I? We are Kohanim (priests); we are from the same family as John the Baptist, but we remained true to the Covenant. How could I ever believe that Yeshua-Jesus was the Messiah? "Everyone" knew that He was a fraud by the way His followers treated my people. However, my heavenly Father, Who drew me unto Himself, had prepared great and wondrous things for me that I never could have imagined.

The Question

"Have you ever given adult consideration to the claim of Christ on your life?" I could not believe it! This guy must be nuts! Can you imagine asking me, someone who is Jewish, if I had ever considered the claims of Christ on my life? Because of Jesus, the Jewish people were persecuted; members of my family suffered and died in the concentration camps. He never could be our long awaited Messiah!

My Early Life

I was born in Brooklyn New York; was circumcised the eighth day; and had a Bar Mitzvah when I was thirteen years old, according to the laws and traditions of our people. While growing up, I attended Sabbath school and morning worship on Saturday mornings. Even though I attended services regularly, I never had inner peace and assurance; nor did I know anyone else who did. While I punctually said my morning and evening prayers, I never experienced real oneness with G-d. I continued in this manner until I was in college and then gradually gave up all prayer and attendance at services. Later, I worked in construction as a cement finisher and eventually went into business in New York City. While I was working as a cement finisher, I met a lovely girl named Judith who was and is the love of my life. We were married sixty-five days later.

Prologue

The Pennsylvania Dutch Country

One spring while I was looking for a vacation spot, a friend told me about the Pennsylvania Dutch Country near Lancaster, Pennsylvania. Judith and I decided to go, and we both fell in love with the area. For many years we vacationed there three or four times a year. In 1968 we were in the area for a weekend, looking for a summer home. While riding through the town of Ronks, we saw a chicken farm for sale. We loved the quiet serene location and knew we wanted to settle there. Meanwhile, my business partner in New York City died unexpectedly, and we decided to sell our share of the business. Judith and I purchased the property in Ronks and built a small motel.

What is The Meaning of Life?

Since my business partner's death, I had started to give more thought to life, more thought to death and more thought to the meaning of life itself. During this period I was troubled with painful back problems and visited Dr. Thomas Berry, a chiropractor in Strasburg, Pennsylvania. Dr. Berry asked me the outrageous question, "Have you ever given adult consideration to the claims of Jesus Christ on your life?" I told him I was Jewish and was not interested in Jesus. After my first visit and his question, I began to study diligently my Tenach (Old Testament Scriptures) again. I would study them incessantly, fall asleep, wake up, and study again. My wife told me that after a few months she thought I was on the verge of losing my mind. After continuing in this condition for some time, I decided that I would settle everything about G-d once and for all.

G-d's Demands

I had always tried to live an ethical life so that I could fulfill G-d's demands. In Leviticus 11:45, G-d says, "Ye shall therefore be holy for I am holy." In 2 Chronicles 7:14 He says, "If my people which are called by my name, shall humble themselves and pray, and seek my face, and turn from their wicked ways; then will I hear from heaven, I will forgive their sin." Isaiah the prophet says, "but your iniquities have separated between you and your G-d and your sins have hid His face from you and He will not hear"(59:2) and Isaiah (64:6) tells us we are all as an unclean thing and all our righteousnesses are as filthy rags. I wondered to myself if it could be that my life was not satisfactory to G-d.

Only One Thing Left to Do

I prayed the following prayer with a broken and contrite heart, for I had to have certain questions answered: "G-d-if there is a G-d-and if you happen to have a Son and if your Son's name is Jesus Christ, will you please reveal Him to me?" Nothing happened-no flashing lights, no ringing bells, nothing absolutely nothing happened. I said to myself, "How stupid can you be, to think something would happen?" So I stopped praying and studying and once again put away the Holy Scriptures. During the next few days, I felt strangely different, but I did not pay much attention to it.

God's Peace

Four or five days later Mr. and Mrs. David Benner of Ronks came to our home. They asked if they could talk to us because they were taking a survey for their church. One of the questions they asked was, "Do you know who Jesus Christ was?" Even though I was not looking at my wife, I could feel her intense stare. She knew what I had thought of Jesus Christ and that I would probably chew up the Benners and spit them out by telling them about the constant abuse the Jewish people received. Instead, I said to them, "Yes I know who He is; He IS the SON of the living G-d." At that immediate moment, peace flowed over me like a river; it was there in an instant, before I even knew it. My Messiah had revealed Himself to me, and now I was one with G-d. Praise His Name! The strange feeling that I had noticed after my prayer and prior to this incident was a change in my thinking. It started with inconsequential things and then moved to more complex. I could sense my whole being, my body, my soul and my mind conforming more and more to the Holy Scripture as the only basis for life, thought and action. In Jeremiah 33:3, YH-H says, "Call unto me and I will answer you and show you great and mighty things which you know not." I did and He did, all glory to His name.

What Does The Jewish Bible Say?

G-d inspired Isaiah to speak of the future in 9:6 "For unto us a child is born, unto us a Son is given and the government shall be upon His shoulder: His name shall be called Wonderful, Counselor, The Mighty God, The Everlasting Father, The Prince of Peace." When I read that for the first time after I had become a believer, I felt as if I previously had been cheated. Suddenly, the Scriptures became alive and took on new meaning. The revelation of the truth of many Scriptures astounded me.

The G-d of Abraham, Isaac and Jacob has a Son. In Proverbs 30:4 it says:

"Who hath ascended up into heaven or descended? Who hath gathered the wind in His fists? Who hath bound the waters in a garment? Who hath established the ends of the earth? What is His name, and what is His SON'S name, if thou canst tell?" (Emphasis added).

The G-d of Abraham, Isaac, and Jacob has a Spirit. Isaiah 48:16 talks of G-d and His Spirit. This clearly shows that the Godhead is composed of more than one. It is a tri-unity.

Our Hearts Must Be Circumcised

We Jewish people must have circumcised hearts and be converted from worldly ways to G-d's ways. Deuteronomy 10:16 says, "Circumcise therefore the foreskin of your heart, be no more stiff necked" (emphasis added). In Ezekiel 18:31 we read, "Cast away from all your transgressions whereby ye have transgressed: and make you a new heart and a new spirit: for why will you die house of Israel?" King David said in Psalm 51:13, "Then will I teach transgressors thy ways; sinners shall be converted unto thee."

A Broken and Contrite Heart Is Not Enough

In addition to a broken and contrite heart, one must have the blood sacrifice of a substitute for the remission of sin. Leviticus, chapter 17:11 teaches, "For the life of the flesh is in the blood and I give it to you upon the altar to make an atonement for your souls: for it is the blood that maketh an atonement for the soul." Exodus chapter 12:5-7, 13, states the same principle. Without the shedding of blood, there can be no remission of sin. The Holy Scriptures have always held the secret. It has been plain for those who would seek it. The Talmud tells us in Yoma 5a that without the shedding of blood there is no remission of sin.

G-d Has Not Forsaken the Jewish People

There is no need for Jewish people to lose heart, for G-d has not forsaken them. In Zechariah 2:8 G-d calls Israel the apple of His eye. In Isaiah, 49:16 G-d says that He has graven Israel on the palms of His hands. Proverbs 3:5-6 tells us, "Trust in the L-RD with all your heart and lean not unto your own understanding. In all thy ways acknowledge Him and He will direct thy paths."

What We Must Do

The prophet Isaiah 1:18 tells us, "Come now and let us reason together saith the L-RD: though your sins be as scarlet they shall be as wool." In Jeremiah 31:31 we learn that the G-d of Abraham, Isaac, and Jacob has promised us (the Jewish people) a New Covenant. This never was fulfilled during the Older Testament period. G-d says that He will remember our sins no more. For Him to do that, we must repent of our sins and claim the sacrifice of Messiah Yeshua -Jesus as our own.

When we accept the provisions of the New Covenant, we, in fact, are accepting the Messiah-ship, sacrifice and lordship of Yeshua the Messiah (Jesus the Anointed One) as binding on our lives. We must follow the precepts enunciated in the New Covenant Scriptures in spirit and in truth. We must serve our Messiah with all our hearts, souls, and minds. He and He alone is the final Pascal Lamb, and His shed blood alone is sufficient to atone for all our sins not just a few sins, but all of our sins, no matter how great or how small.

Jeremiah explains the New Covenant in 31:31. In the Holy Scriptures, the prophet Joel says in chapter 2:12-13, 32 "Therefore also now, saith the L-RD, turn ye even to me with all your heart, with fasting, with weeping, and with mourning. Rend your heart, not your garments, turn unto the L-RD your G-d: for He is gracious, merciful, slow to anger, of great kindness and repents Him of the evil … And it shall come to pass that whosoever shall call on the name of the L-RD shall be delivered: for in Mt. Zion and in Jerusalem shall be deliverance as the L-RD hath said in the remnant whom the L-RD shall call" (emphasis added). I beg you brethren; call on the L-rd; see if you are one of the remnant of Israel of whom He speaks, one of those who will be saved from the lake of the everlasting burnings.

One Greater Than Moses

Even as Moses was the deliverer of our people from bondage in Egypt, our G-d promised that one greater than Moses was to come. G-d speaks to Moses in Deuteronomy 18:18-19 "I will raise them up a Prophet from among their brethren, like unto thee, and put my words in His mouth: He shall speak unto them, all that I shall command him ... and it shall come to pass whosoever will not harken unto my words, which He shall speak in my name, I will require it of him." Brethren, do not make the same mistake our ancestors did in rejecting our Messiah. Messiah has come and He has fulfilled hundreds of predictions made in our Scriptures concerning His coming and His work.

You Can Be Redeemed

In Jeremiah 31:35-36, the prophet tells us that Israel will always be a nation before our God. This does not mean the country Israel, but the Hebrew people. I beseech you; claim the New Covenant and the promises made in Jeremiah 31:31 and following. Pray the prayer I prayed, and ask God to open your eyes and your heart. Try Him; see if He shows you great and mighty things, which you know not. The prophet Ezekiel asks why will you die, Oh house of Israel? He instructs, "Seek the L-RD while He may be found" (55: 6). Hosea 14:1 says, "Return, O Israel, unto the L-RD thy G-d; for thou has stumbled in thine inequity." Ecclesiastes 7:20 tells us "There is not a just man upon earth that doeth good and sinneth not." In Psalm 116:13, King David said "I will take the cup of salvation and call upon the name of the L-RD." What ABOUT YOU?

Redemption Draws Near

Call on our Heavenly Father and see if He showers you with spiritual blessings from Heaven, even more blessings than you can endure! Will you call on the Jewish Messiah, The L-rd Yeshua? He is bone of our bone and flesh of our flesh. He came to pay the price for your sins so that you could be one with our Heavenly Father. Flee from the wrath to come! Do not reject Him. If you do, you will be under his contempt (Dan. 12:2) and will spend eternity (not one or five years, but forever) with all the evil people who have hated the Jewish people since the beginning of our nation. Call on Him now! The people who used Christ's name to do evil to the Hebrew people will receive just punishment for their deeds. Do not wind up in the same place as they will. In the New Testament in Matthew 7:21-23, our Messiah says He will say to these people, "Depart from me, I never knew you." They will go to the lake of the everlasting burnings.

Our Messiah says in the New Testament in John 14:6, "I am the way, the truth and the life, no man cometh unto the Father but by me." In Romans 10:9 we read, "If thou shalt confess with thy mouth the L-rd Jesus the Messiah and shall believe in thine heart that G-d hath raised Him from the dead, thou shalt be saved." If you do not have the faith to believe, ask the Almighty One to supply it to you. He will show you great and mighty things, which you know not. Remember, the grass withers, the flower fades, but the word of G-d shall stand forever (Isaiah 40:8).

Conclusion:

Dear reader, I must ask you some questions: What part of the body of Messiah are you? Are you a part of the group that says El-him-G-d is finished with Israel? Do you say that Israel had her chance; now it is our turn? Or do you say it really does not matter, because El-him will have mercy on whom He will have mercy, and harden whom He will harden?

The Scripture says that the L-rd Messiah wept over Jerusalem. I submit to you that He did not once weep, but that He weeps for her very often. He wept over her from their first rebellion, and He continues to weep over her to this very day.

Paul in Romans 11:5 tells us that there is a remnant of Israel chosen by grace. The rest were given the spirit of stupor so that the Gentiles could come in to make Israel envious. If you are a believing Gentile, you are a wild olive branch that was grafted into the natural olive tree (Romans 11:17). The Holy Spirit, through the apostle Paul, tells you not to be high-minded. There will come a time when all Israel will be saved. Are you going to take part in that harvest, or are you going to sit on the sidelines?

Can you be complacent when your bridegroom is weeping? Is your heart so hard that it has no compassion for those for whom He weeps? I am not saying that He weeps only for Israel. I am saying among those for whom He weeps are those people whom He has preserved to this day, while their ancient enemies have vanished.

Do you pray for the salvation of the seed of Israel? Do you witness to her? Do you give financial support to Jewish missions and missionaries? What do you do, now that you are a new creation in the Jewish Messiah, to bring the natural descendants of Abraham into our Father's kingdom?

One of the feasts which we will study is the holiday of Shemini Atzeret. It symbolizes the new creation and is fulfilled in the sacrifice of Yeshua the Messiah. This is the first day of a believer's new life. Now is the chance to put everything right and get back on track.

Isaiah has a specific command to those who would follow G-d. In 58:1ff, he writes, "Shout aloud, do not hold back. Raise your voice like a trumpet. Declare to my people their rebellion and to the house of Jacob their sins. For day after day they seek me out; they seem eager to know my ways, as if they were a nation that does what is right and has not forsaken the commands of its G-d."

According to the New Covenant described in Jeremiah 31:31ff, the descendants of Israel are a nation before El-him for as long as the sun gives light by day and the moon and the stars give light by night. Only if Heaven can be measured and the foundations of the earth beneath searched out will Israel ever be cast off for what she has done, says the L-rd. Matthew tells us in 28:19, "therefore go and make disciples of all nations [which includes individual Jewish people], baptizing them in the name of the Father the Son and the Holy Spirit."

This convocation, Shemini Atzeret, speaks of the sufficiency of the final sacrifice of Messiah Yeshua. He suffered so that all who would repent of their sins, would come to Him for salvation, and would spend eternity with Him in heaven. Each of us will have to give an account for the things we did and did not do while we were on this earth. I implore you: do not be found wanting when the balances are weighed regarding your witness to Israel. Beloved, pray for the peace of Jerusalem and salvation of the remnant from the lost sheep of the house of Israel. Jewish missions are in need of not only prayer support but financial support also. The apostle to the Gentiles tells us in Romans 15:27 "For if the Gentiles have shared in the Jews' spiritual blessings, they owe it to the Jews to share with them their material blessings." To Jeh-vah El-him goes all the glory.

EPILOGUE

All the convocations in Leviticus were a part of the grand plan of our G-d to show men that they were sinful people in need of something external to themselves for salvation. The Levitical convocations in their entirety were designed to give glory to El-him. By complying with the law and these convocations, some of the people of the nation of Israel were showing their inability to be acceptable to El-him without the prescribed sacrifices. The law was Israel's schoolmaster to bring her to Messiah, that she might be justified by faith (Galatians 3:24 [KJV]).

When born-again believers celebrate these convocations, they are to be careful that they celebrate them in the fullness of completion and fulfillment in Messiah Yeshua-Jesus. They are biblically ordained holidays that El-him has put in place for His own glory. They are no more obsolete than belief in Yeshua the Messiah would be obsolete. Our glory is not in the sacrifices, but in the One who completed the final sacrifice for our salvation. Each holiday we celebrate brings out a different aspect of that salvation.

When Elijah was in the mountain, he told G-d that he was the only one left in Israel who was still faithful to Him. G-d told Elijah that there were seven thousand who had not bowed the knee to Baal. My calculations indicate that would mean that only one-half of one percent of all the people of the nation of Israel living at that time would go into El-him's spiritual kingdom, for they alone had refrained from idol worship. The people who saw the eternal kingdom of Messiah were very few compared to the number of people in the nation of Israel.

Idol worshipers or anyone else who sinned defiantly blasphemed the L-rd. Numbers 15:30 says that those people must be cut off from G-d's people. That does not mean they would be thrown out of Israel, but it does mean that they would not see the eternal kingdom, unless they repented and went directly to El-him to receive forgiveness. Under the law of Moses there is no provision for forgiveness for intentional sins.

During the times of the Temple, there were common people, spiritual leaders, and civil rulers-Pharisees, Sadducees, Nazarites, Essenes, zealots, and many other different groups existing at the same time. Each had different ideas as to what would get them into G-d's eternal Kingdom.

Today, we are in the same position that ancient Israel was. We have many people who say they are "Christians" and that they belong to the kingdom of Jesus. They look on the natural creation and not the spiritual creation. We have common people with no particular denominational affiliation; Evangelicals, Fundamentalists, Liberals, Pentecostals, and over one-thousand different cults… all with different ideas of what will get them into G-d's eternal kingdom.

The Jewish people assumed that they had spiritual salvation because Abraham was their Father, and Isaac and Jacob were their ancestors. Many people today think that just because they know about Jesus, they are going to inherit eternal life with Him in Heaven; yet nothing could be further from the truth. Just as the majority of Israelites were deceived regarding their eternal salvation, I submit to you that the majority of those calling themselves "Christian" are likewise deceived.

As an ambassador to the Jewish people and a spiritual leader, I will share two specific incidents with you that are typical of what exists in "Christianity". The first involves a printer that we used for our printing needs from time to time. He knew that I was Jewish and that I was a believer. Whenever I saw him, he would immediately start to talk about Judaism. I witnessed to him on a couple of occasions, and at one time I decided I was going to nail things down. He told me that he had been a Christian for a long time. I pressed him again and asked him how long. He kept avoiding the point and finally I put it to him, in no uncertain terms, "How long have you been a Christian?" He said to me, "I have been a Christian for a long, long time; I was born a Christian." Well dear reader, that is just a little bit too long. One has to make a personal decision.

The second incident does not involve an individual, but a congregation. The Messianic Hebrew Christian Fellowship had put advertisements in our local newspapers stating that we would be willing to teach a Sunday school class for a quarter or longer in any church on the topic "An Introduction to the Jewish Scriptures that lead to Salvation." One church that we had gone into recommended that we go to another church of the same denomination. One Sunday, about two thirds through the quarter, I was teaching the course. When I was finished, a gentleman came up to me and told me that he was seventy two years old and was now retired. He had been a pastor in that denomination his entire adult life. He said to me, "I realize what you are teaching is purely scriptural, but I have never heard these things you are talking about. I was never taught about them in seminary, and I never taught them to any congregation that I led." He then asked if he could have a copy of the notes for the whole series. My subject matter that day dealt with the necessity of the new birth: "old things must pass away and behold all things must become new" (2 Cor. 5:17). I also dealt with the fact that a blood atonement had to be applied to an individual for that person to receive salvation. I finished by showing that salvation was an individual occurrence; there had to be a personal vertical relationship between the sinner and El-him.

Three months after finishing that course, we received a call from the assistant pastor of that particular congregation. He asked if we would come back and teach some more, because the congregation was terribly troubled; many of the members did not believe that they had eternal life. We told them that we would gladly come back. I wondered where the pastor was in all of this. What were their elders doing? What were their teachers teaching? We gave abundant praise to El-him, thanking Him for using us to bring His light to that congregation.

As in Jeremiah's day there now is a famine of God's word in the land. What the world calls the church of Jesus the Messiah is not the true Church. It does not understand the concept of being born again into a spiritual kingdom. Just as vast numbers of Israel were deceived, so also vast numbers of what we call the church are deceived. It seems that there is a latent pattern of thought inside great numbers of people that tells them that since the Almighty eternal G-d gave them natural life, He is obliged also to give them spiritual life with Him in Heaven. Nothing could be further from the truth.

Regarding the kingdom of heaven, Messiah Yeshua- Jesus said, "They will say unto me L-rd, L-rd I will tell them, depart from me I never knew you" (Matt. 7: 21-23). Scripture is clear: wide is the road and broad is the gate that leads to destruction and many there are who will find it. We are also told that narrow is the road and straight is the gate to eternal life and few there are who will find it (Matt. 7:13-14).

Israel will not get to Heaven merely because the Lord Almighty gave her the law; those who call themselves Christians will not get into Heaven merely because they call themselves Christians. They must have a Spiritual new birth. Fulfilling the law never saved one Israelite, because no one except Messiah was able to fulfill the law's requirements. Believing in the historical Jesus and belonging to a congregation where one's parents and/or grandparents had or have membership will not save one person who claims to be a Christian. The Scripture is clear that you must be born again and that your spirit must bear witness with G-d's Spirit that you are His child (Rom. 8:16). Without the new spiritual birth, no one, whether Jew or Gentile, will see the kingdom of heaven.

I mention all of this and submit to you the following: take G-d's own convocations, which belong to every believer and not to Israel alone, and celebrate them to and for the glory of Messiah Jesus. Designate your worship day that occurs nearest to the date of each one of the Levitical feasts, review the feasts, and show how Messiah has fulfilled them. Demonstrate your obligations to Him as His followers to strive for holiness, righteousness, mercy, peace, and love. Separate yourselves from the foolishness of manmade religion, and cleave unto the author and finisher of our faith.

May we all be pleased to see Yeshua-Jesus the Messiah high and lifted up, initiating great revival in our time for His own honor and glory.

Passover

INTRODUCTION

According to Jewish authority, Passover is the oldest celebrated holiday on the face of this earth. It was instituted by our Creator and is a remembrance of how He saved His people when they were in one of their darkest hours. Passover is an occasion of great joy, happiness, and anticipation. It is a time when Jewish families get together and remember one of our Creators greatest acts of kindness and displays of His awesome power. The wonderful deliverance from Egypt is relived, and hearts are again filled with praise to The L-rd our G-d.

The historical Passover celebration consists of two parts--the sacrifice of a lamb or goat kid and the feast when that animal is eaten. The Passover sacrificial lamb that was to provide deliverance for the children of Israel in Egypt had to be a perfect lamb without any defects. It was sacrificed at twilight on the 14th day of the month of Abib which was later renamed Nisan (March-April). The actual Passover meal using the slain lamb was eaten after sundown, which was the start of the 15th day. The 15th day began the seven-day Feast of Unleavened Bread. There was to be no work on the first day and no work on the last day, as they were both holy Sabbaths. Passover is a reminder of our Father our King's care and faithfulness to the descendants of Jacob. Passover has always been a sustaining influence for Jacob's posterity during its times of tribulation, holocaust and heartache.

The Passover service is called a Seder, and historically it has been conducted in the home. In the last century the tradition of joining together to celebrate Passover in a Jewish Center or hotel has become quite popular. This is usually done on the second night. It is done on the first night only when family units cannot get together. When older people retire and move to retirement communities, very often these communities are not in close proximity to their families; and celebrating Passover in the retirement community dining room or social hall is like celebrating with an extended family.

The Seder is held at the evening meal after sundown. During the day the men go to the Synagogue for prayer and a service, while the women cook and prepare the food. As a child, this was a very special time in my life. I was the only male grandchild, and I spent the day with my grandfather. There were just the two of us with no interruptions. We would talk about life and our duty as Jews to serve our fellow man as well as the L-rd our G-d. There would come a certain time in our conversation when my grandfather would talk about his early years in Russia and the persecution he received (from those who called themselves Christians) because he was Jewish. He held no animosity toward anyone but had only love for his fellow man and his King.

Later in the day he would say to me, "I think it's time we go to the Synagogue and pray." When anyone walked into the Synagogue after the service had started, all we would see was a sea of men wearing their Yarmulkes (skull caps head coverings) and their prayer shawls. There was not a chance I could find my father. After our time of prayer it was time to go home and make sure that everything was ready for the celebration of the Passover.

There is not a day that goes by that I do not think of my grandparents. They always tried to follow the law our heavenly Father gave to Moses, as we are a family of Kohanim (descendants of the priesthood). In spite of their sincerity, they never came to know Y'shua the Messiah who is the author and finisher of our faith. When I think of their final abode, I feel an agony in my soul. I identify with Paul's heartfelt lament in Romans 10:1-4. I often feel great pain in my heart, as I seek to share the gospel of Yeshua with the lost and remember my own grandparents who were just as lost. In the end, I know that my Redeemer lives and that He does all things right, according to the counsel of His own will. To those of you who may mourn for your own loved ones, remember that Yeshua will wipe away every one of our tears when we see Him face to face.

In all we say and do as believers, we are to give Messiah Yeshua – (Jesus) honor and glory. While I always enjoyed celebrating Passover in my youth, it does not compare with the joy of celebrating it now. In my youth we celebrated the deliverance from Egypt and looked forward to the coming of Elijah to announce Messiah. When I celebrate Passover now, joy overwhelms me as I remember that Messiah has come; and by His death He has given me spiritual redemption, which is far better than mere physical redemption.

Messiah raised Passover to a higher level by using His last Passover while on earth to give believers the Lord's Supper so that we may receive constant joy and strength from Him each and every day of our lives. We will explore the aspect of gaining joy and strength through the Passover/Lord's Supper by the means of three questions, their answers, and a conclusion.

THREE QUESTIONS AND THEIR ANSWERS

How and when was Passover established?

How was and is Passover celebrated?

What are the implications of Passover under the New Covenant?

How and when was Passover established?

Leviticus 23 records the list of Israel's feasts. The first one listed (verse 3) is the seventh-day Sabbath. The next one is the Lord's Passover: "These are the Lord's appointed feasts, the sacred assemblies you are to proclaim at their appointed times: our Father's ordained Passover begins at twilight on the fourteenth day of the first month" (vs. 4-5).

Exodus 12:1-16 records the first Passover night. Let us read again the inspired description of that amazing night.

Our Creator the L-rd G-d said to Moses and Aaron in Egypt, "This month is to be for you the first month, the first month of your year. Tell the whole community of Israel that on the tenth day of this month each man is to take a lamb for his family, one for each household. If any household is too small for a whole lamb, they must share one with their nearest neighbor, having taken into account the number of people there are. You are to determine the amount of lamb needed in accordance with what each person will eat.

The animals you choose must be year old males without defect, and you may take them from the sheep or the goats. Take care of them until the fourteenth day of the month, when all the people of the community of Israel must slaughter them at twilight.

Then they are to take some of the blood and put it on the sides and top of the door frames of the houses where they eat the lambs. That same night they are to eat the meat roasted over the fire, along with bitter herbs, and bread made without yeast. Do not eat the meat raw or cooked in water, but roast it over the fire head, legs and inner parts. Do not leave any of it till morning; if some is left till morning, you must burn it.

This is how you are to eat it: with your cloak tucked into your belt, your sandals on your feet and your staff in your hand. Eat it in haste; it is the L-rd's Passover. On that same night I will pass through Egypt and strike down every firstborn both men and animals and I will bring judgment on all the gods of Egypt.

I am you're the L-rd your G-d. The blood will be a sign for you on the houses where you are; and when I see the blood, I will pass over you. No destructive plague will touch you when I strike Egypt. This is a day you are to commemorate; for the generations to come you shall celebrate it as a festival to the L-ord – a lasting ordinance.

For seven days you are to eat bread made without yeast. On the first day remove the yeast from your houses, for whoever eats anything with yeast in it from the first day through the seventh must be cut off from Israel. On the first day hold a sacred assembly, and another one on the seventh day. Do no work at all on these days, except to prepare food for everyone to eat – that is all you may do. Exodus 12:40-49 gives some specific history and provides explicit regulations that were to be followed in the Passover observance.

Now the length of time that the Israelite people lived in Egypt was 430 years. At the end of the 430 years, to the very day, all the Israelite's divisions left Egypt. Because our Father our Creator kept vigil that night to bring them out of Egypt, on this night all the Israelites are to keep vigil to honor Him for the generations to come.

The Lord said to Moses and Aaron, "These are the regulations for Passover: No foreigner is to eat of it. Any slave you have bought may eat of it after you have circumcised him, but a temporary resident and a hired worker may not eat of it. It must be eaten inside the house; take none of the meat outside the house. Do not break any of the bones. The whole community of Israel must celebrate it.

An alien living among you who wants to celebrate our Father's Passover must have all the males in his household circumcised; then he may take part like one born in the land. No uncircumcised male may eat of it. The same law applies to the native-born and to the alien living among you."

Numbers 9:10 gives a few more instructions. "Tell the Israelites: 'When any of you or your descendants are unclean because of a dead body or are away on a journey, they may still celebrate the Lord's Passover. They are to celebrate on the fourteenth day of the second month at twilight.'"

Passover was established by our Father Himself, at the time when He delivered Israel from the oppression of Egypt. It was designed to be a commemorative feast, with specific rules for who was to partake, what was to be eaten, how the food was to be prepared and eaten, and where it was to be eaten.

How was and is Passover celebrated?

Each time the Passover is celebrated it is celebrated as a memorial to the original Passover that occurred in Egypt. Over the years the service has changed, but the basic elements have remained the same. The basic elements on the table (post-temple destruction period) are as follows: matzo, salt water, shank bone of a lamb, horseradish, parsley, roasted egg, horseradish root, wine, and charoset. The Talmud encourages a long service, saying that it gives glory to the L-rd for His great and wondrous salvation. The average Passover service will last approximately four hours. Very often the leader of the service wears a white robe called a kittel. Wearing white symbolizes the leader's role as priest of the home. The wearing of the kittle and the designation of the father or leader as priest of the home came into being after the destruction of the temple and the disbanding of the priestly function of sacrifice.

The Passover service is not only joyful; it is also very serious. It is to be celebrated with both a happy heart and a reverent attitude. The story is to be passed on from generation to generation to celebrate the goodness of the L-rd to His chosen people. And you shall tell your son in that day, saying: "it is because of that which the L-rd did for me when I came for out of Egypt that we have this celebration." Each person is to celebrate the Passover as if he himself was coming out from Egypt.

The Passover service is called a Seder. Seder is a Hebrew word meaning "order" and, as would be expected, there is a definite order to the service. It is conducted from a book called the Haggadah, which means "to tell" and is used to tell the story of the Passover. Instead of one standard Haggadah for every family to use during the service, there are over twelve hundred different ones in print. There are frequent new publications of the Haggadah that place a special emphasis on aspects that were not highlighted before.

I have formulated an expanded service for Passover that we originally used at the Messianic Hebrew Christian Fellowship. It not only includes the rabbinic interpretations of the symbols used during the service, but it also highlights the fulfillment by Messiah as explained in the New Covenant Scriptures.

The Seder plate is placed in the center of the table and contains the main symbols of this service: the shank bone of a lamb, horseradish and horseradish root, a roasted egg, parsley, and charoset (a mixture of chopped apples, honey, dates, and cinnamon). In addition to the Seder plate, there is another plate that contains three matzos wrapped in a special cloth. There are also a few bowls of salt water for the dipping of vegetables and glasses of wine or grape juice denoting the four promises given to Israel. The explanation for the symbols comes out of rabbinic Judaism.

The first symbol is the three MATZOS, commemorating the bread which our forefathers were compelled to eat during their hasty departure from Egypt. Rabbinic Judaism explains that the three matzos represent the three religious groupings of the Jewish people: Kohen, Levi, and Yisrael. The matzos are placed together on a plate and wrapped with a cloth to indicate the unity of the Jewish people. In unity, we find our strength and power to survive. In reality, the rabbis do not really know why there are three matzos on the plate.

The second symbol is the ROASTED SHANKBONE, which reminds us of the Paschal lamb, a special animal sacrifice which our ancestors offered on the altar of the great Temple in Jerusalem on the Passover holiday.

The third symbol is a ROASTED EGG, which reminds us of a second offering brought to the Temple on Passover. It was known as the FESTIVAL OFFERING, for it was brought on each of the three Festivals

Pesach, Shavuot and Sukkot (Passover, the Feast of Weeks and the Feast of Tabernacles).

The fourth symbol is the MOROR, the bitter-herbs, which reminds us of the bitterness of slavery which our ancestors were compelled to endure.

The fifth symbol is the CHAROSES, made to resemble mortar, used at this time to remind us of the mortar with which our forefathers made bricks for the building of Egyptian cities.

The final symbol is the KARPAS, a green vegetable, used to remind us that Pesach coincides with the arrival of spring and the gathering of the spring harvest. Passover in ancient times was also an agricultural festival and an occasion on which our ancestors gave thanks for the earth's rich bounties.

In addition to the Seder plate, each adult has a glass of wine or grape juice in front of him. There is also grape juice for children. This is a very important part of the service, as it symbolizes the L-rd's four-fold promise to Israel. The bowls of salt water are to symbolize the Red Sea as well as the tears of the children of Israel.

The Passover is not only celebrated by Jewish people who follow Rabbinic Judaism, but it is also celebrated by Messianic congregations that are comprised of born-again Jewish people as well as born-again Gentiles. Remember that our Messiah Yeshua the Righteous one celebrated the Passover with His disciples on the night He was betrayed.

What are the implications of Passover under the New Covenant?

The implications of Passover under the New Covenant are quite startling. I would like to make some comments concerning the Passover and how its symbols affect me as a believer.

In the center of the table are the three matzos wrapped in the unity bag. They remind me of the triune Godhead. There are not three separate entities, but one monotheistic deity composed of three separate entities as "Echad" in the Shema "one comprised of more than one". We read the following in Isaiah 48:16; "Come near me and listen to this: 'From the first announcement I have not spoken in secret; at the time it happens, I am there.' And now the Sovereign L-rd has sent me [Messiah], with His Spirit" (the tri-unity).

The salt water used in the service reminds me of the tears Yeshua shed when He wept over Jerusalem (Luke 19:41).

The glass of wine symbolizes the shed blood of our Messiah. It was needful for him to shed His blood only once. It is done; and now, after shedding that blood, He sits at the right hand of our Heavenly Father.

When the parsley is dipped in salt water, it reminds me that in my new life, I must be salt and light. When I eat the bitter herbs (as the rabbis say, until tears come to my eyes), I remember the bitterness of my own sin and the cost to Messiah to pay for it. I am reminded of the deceitfulness of my own heart. Jeremiah 17:9 tells us that the heart is deceitful above all things and desperately wicked and asks who can know it.

When I see the shank bone, I am reminded of the perfect sacrifice of Yeshua the Messiah. Romans 8:1 tells us; "There is therefore now no condemnation to those who are in Christ Jesus [Messiah Yeshua], who do not walk according to the flesh, but according to the Spirit".

In Egypt the lamb was killed, the blood was applied, and the people received salvation in the natural sense. Under the New Covenant this holiday, given to Israel to celebrate in the natural realm, becomes a celebration for believers in the spiritual realm. A believer in Messiah Yeshua is a new creation; old things have passed away; behold all things have become new (2 Cor. 5:17). Messiah Yeshua was sacrificed on Calvary's Cross. His blood paid for all the sins of all people who would come to Him for salvation. (I John 2:2)

I Corinthians 5:6ff beautifully lays out this holiday and its implications for a New Covenant believer. "Your boasting is not good. Don't you know that a little yeast works through the whole batch of dough? Get rid of the old yeast that you may be a new batch without yeast—as you really are. For Messiah, our Passover lamb, has been sacrificed. Therefore let us keep the Festival, not with the old yeast, the yeast of malice and wickedness, but with bread without yeast, the bread of sincerity and truth."

For believers, this holiday is not something that is celebrated just one evening out of the year. Because of the sacrifice of Messiah and His shed blood this holiday celebration is to affect our ways and lives for the entire year. Messiah our Passover is to be before us -- not only every day, but every hour and every minute of our lives. No one can ever earn Messiah's salvation; it is a free gift. Because we received this free gift, we are responsible to the Giver of the gift to yield to His ways and to suppress our own natural inclinations.

A dear friend of mine, Bishop Albert Belton, asked me to speak at the congregation he pastors. In honor of the occasion, the congregation sang a song that comes from the island of Jamaica.

You don't have to slay the lamb anymore.

You don't have to put the blood on the door.

Someone has taken the place of the Lamb.

He is the great I am.

He is the great I am.

He is the great I am.

Someone has taken the place of the Lamb.

He is the great I am.

That says it all!

I have some questions for you. Are you covered by the blood and righteousness of Yeshua the Messiah? Hebrews 9:22, referring to Leviticus 17:11, says, "Without the shedding of blood there is no remission of sin." Have your sins been forgiven? Are they removed as far as the east is from the west (Psalms. 103:12), or are you still in your sins?

In Egypt our Heavenly Father's Spirit passed over the huts of the people where the blood was applied. Some huts had no blood; the people inside them did not believe. They thought the whole thing would not happen. But it did happen, and their firstborn were struck down. No one prevented them from applying the blood, but they chose not to; and they suffered the consequences.

If you are not reborn of the Spirit of our Creator, I ask you, are you not tired of your own sin yet? Are you not weary? Just as the gods of the Egyptians failed them, yours will fail you if you are not one with Messiah. If at any time you feel the urging of the Holy Spirit calling on you to repent, the Scriptures tell you to believe on Yeshua the Messiah and you will be saved. John 1:29 tells us: "Behold! The Lamb of God who takes away the sin of the world!".

He is my Savior. Is He yours?

He is my King. Is He yours?

He is my Master and my Bridegroom. Is He yours?

The world was created by Him and for Him. Seek Him while He may be found. Call on Him while He is still near. Repent of your sin with a broken and contrite heart, and believe on Him, and you will receive salvation. If you just can't believe on Him, ask our creator to reveal to you if He has sent a Savior, and also reveal to you who He is.

If you are a believer, the Lord has four promises for you:

Acts 2:21 everyone who calls on the name of the L-rd will receive salvation.

James 4:8 Come near to our L-rd and He will come near to you.

Revelation 3:20 - Here I am! I stand at the door and knock. If anyone hears my voice and opens the door, I will go in and eat with him, and he with Me.

Hebrews 7:25 - Therefore He is able to save completely those who come to the L-rd through Him because He always lives to intercede for them.

May the words of our mouth and the meditations of our heart be acceptable to you, our rock and our Redeemer.

Outline for the seder service

The explanations given are a refresher to those who have celebrated the Passover before as well as instructions to those who have not. Anyone who wishes to celebrate the Passover may do so using the

Passover   49

following outline. All who do so will relive both that awesome Passover night and the even more awesome event of Calvary. The comments that follow my name (LLOYD) come from the rabbinic Haggadah of our choice, and the comments that follow my wife's name (JUDITH) are the New Covenant fulfillment of the traditions of the Passover

LLOYD: "When our Creator commanded the children of Israel to leave Egypt, He commanded them to eat only unleavened bread with the Passover meal, which was eaten the night before they left Egypt. For seven days no yeast is to be found in your houses. And whoever eats anything with yeast in it must be cut off from the community of Israel, whether he is an alien or native-born. Eat nothing made with yeast. Wherever you live, you must eat unleavened bread" (Exodus 12:19, 20).

Preparing the house for Passover puts a special burden upon the family. In the days before the Passover celebration the house is thoroughly cleaned. Floors, walls and ceilings are scrubbed. Pots, pans and utensils are boiled; and plates and glassware are washed in very hot water. This is done to insure that there is no leaven in the house.

As part of the tradition that is followed when the husband returns from the Synagogue, he will search his house for leaven. The wife usually makes this very easy for him by putting some bread crumbs on the side of the counter or the stove. Once the husband finds the leaven, he sweeps it into a wooden spoon with a feather. Then it is either burned (in the orthodox tradition) or thrown away (in the tradition of the rest of Judaism).

JUDITH: "Yeshua sent Peter and John, saying 'Go and make preparations for us to eat the Passover.' 'Where do you want us to prepare for it?' they asked. He replied, 'As you enter the city, a man carrying a jar of water will meet you. Follow him to the house that he enters, and say to the owner of the house,' The teacher asks: 'Where is the guest room, where I may eat the Passover with my disciples?' He will show you a large upper room, all furnished. Make preparations there'." (Luke 22: 8-12)

Let us search out the leaven of sin in our lives, and so let us keep the feast of unleavened bread, the Passover as it is written "But let a man examine himself, and so let him eat of that bread, and drink of that cup".

LLOYD: At this point the actual service begins with the lady of the house lighting the Passover candles. Tradition tells us that the woman lights the candles because the women of the generation that left Egypt were more righteous than the men.

JUDITH: Blessed art thou, Avinu Malkenu (our Father, our King), who has sanctified us by thy grace and has permitted us to kindle festival lights. Blessed art thou, our Father, King of the universe, who has kept us in life and has preserved us and has enabled us to reach this Passover season. As the woman begins the Seder and gives light to the Passover table, so it was from the seed of a woman the Messiah came to perform His redemptive ministry and bring light to the world. As it is written: "The people living in darkness have seen a great light; on those living in the land of the shadow of death a light has dawned" (Matt. 4:16).

LLOYD: As we read through the Haggadah, we see the fruit of the vine is consumed four times. These four cups stand for the four 'I Wills' recorded in Exodus 6:6, 7.

One: THE CUP OF SANCTIFICATION represents the promise: "I will bring you out from under the burdens of the Egyptians."

Two: THE CUP OF JUDGMENT represents the promise: "I will rid you out of their bondage."

Three: THE CUP OF REDEMPTION represents the promise: "I will redeem you with an outstretched arm."

Four: THE CUP OF PRAISE: represents the promise "I will take you to me for a people."

At this point in the service the leader raises the first cup of wine and says the following:

The first cup is the cup of sanctification which represents the first "I WILL" - I will bring you out from under the burdens of the Egyptians."

JUDITH: And by the first promise, we who have been redeemed have been made holy (sanctified) through the sacrifice of the body of Yeshua the Messiah, once for all (Heb. 10:10).

LLOYD: Please raise your glass of wine and repeat the blessing after me." (Everyone raises the first cup and repeats the blessing after me).

Blessed art thou, O Eternal, Our Creator, King of the Universe, creator of the fruit of the vine. Blessed art thou, our Creator, ruler of the world, who chose us out of all the people and selected us over all of the nations, and made us holy through Your commandments.

Urchatz (washing of the hands):

At this point in the Seder, in traditional Jewish homes, the mother goes around the table holding a bowl of water in which everyone washes his hands"

JUDITH: As New Testament believers, each of us will hold the bowl of water while the person sitting next to us washes his hands. Then that person can do the same for the next person; in this way, each of us will act as a servant to our neighbor.

Concerning the washing, it is written:

It was just before the Passover Feast. Yeshua knew that the time had come for Him to leave this world and go to the Father. Having loved His own who were in the world, He now showed them the full extent of His love. The evening meal was being served, and the devil had already prompted Judas Iscariot, son of Simon, to betray Jesus [Messiah].

Yeshua the Messiah knew that the Father had put all things under His power, and that He had come from the Father and was returning to the Father our Creator; so He got up from the meal, took off his outer clothing, and wrapped a towel around His waist. After that, He poured water into a basin and began to wash His disciples' feet, drying them with the towel that was wrapped around Him.

He came to Simon Peter, who said to Him, "Master, are you going to wash my feet?" Yeshua replied, "You do not realize now what I am doing, but later you will understand." "No," said Peter, "you shall never wash my feet."

Yeshua answered, "Unless I wash you, you have no part with me." "Then, Simon Peter replied, "not just my feet but my hands and my head as well!" Yeshua answered, "A person who has had a bath needs only to wash his feet; his whole body is clean. And you are clean, though not every one of you."

Yeshua the Messiah did more than what was required. Since the lowest position in the household was to wash the feet of guests entering the house Yeshua welcomes His disciples into His Father's house by washing their feet. He came to serve others, giving us an example to follow.

LLOYD: Karpas (dipping of greens in salt water):

At this point, the greens are dipped in the salt water. The blessing is said and everyone eats the parsley. "Blessed art thou, oh L-rd our G-d King of the Universe, Creator of the fruits of the earth."

Yachutz (breaking of the middle matzo):

The unleavened bread (matzo) is found in a special tri-sectioned cloth bag called a Unity. The matzos in the first and third compartments are left alone, and the matzo from the middle compartment is removed and broken in half. One piece is returned to the unity bag and the other piece is wrapped in a linen napkin. It is hidden by the leader and is called the "Afikomen." This Afikomen later becomes an important part of the Seder service.

JUDITH: The unity is representational of our Creator, a unique unity, manifested in three persons: Father, Son, and Holy Spirit. The Afikomen symbolizes the broken body of our Messiah! After it is broken, it is wrapped in linen and hidden away. The children search for the Afikomen and then bring it back to the leader of the Seder, who must redeem it.

LLOYD: Exodus 12 tells us how the L-rd our G-d redeemed His people from Egypt by His mighty power. Literally, Passover is a story of redemption by the shedding of the blood of the Passover Lamb.

JUDITH: It is the story of death, of life, and of resurrection. Essentially it has the elements as the gospel. It is the blood that makes atonement for the soul (Leviticus 17:11). And so, the L-rd G-d taught us to keep the Passover as a memorial feast of the physical salvation which He wrought in Egypt, and to keep the Messiah's Passover in memory of the spiritual salvation which He bought for us with His own life.

LLOYD: "On the table, there is another plate of matzo that has a white cloth over it. The matzos are uncovered and the leader of the Seder lifts up the matzo container and recites the following with feeling. "This is the bread of affliction which our ancestors ate in the land of Egypt; Let those who are hungry, enter and eat. Let all who are in need come and celebrate the Passover. Many today are enslaved by sin and many by oppressors. May all be made free through Messiah."

THE FOUR QUESTIONS:

This is a standard section in the service. It is always called The Four Questions even though many Haggadahs contain more than four questions in this section. In this service, I have included five questions.

During the service, the youngest member of the family asks the Leader four questions. The reason the youngest member of the family is chosen is so that everyone will get a chance to ask the questions at Passover. Every child is the youngest at least once."

CHILD: Why is this night different from all other nights?

LLOYD: I am glad you asked this question. This night is different from all other nights, because on this night we celebrate the going forth of the Jewish people from slavery into freedom. We were slaves to Pharaoh in Egypt, and the Lord redeemed us with a mighty hand.

CHILD: On all other nights we may eat leavened or unleavened bread; why is it that on this night we eat only unleavened bread?

LLOYD: When Pharaoh let our forefathers go from Egypt they were forced to flee in great haste. They had no time to bake their bread and could not wait for the yeast to rise. The sun beat down on the dough as they carried it along, and baked it into unleavened bread called matzo.

CHILD: Why do we eat bitter herbs tonight?

LLOYD: Because our forefathers were slaves in Egypt and their lives were made very bitter."

CHILD: Why do we dip the herbs twice tonight?

LLOYD: We dip the parsley in salt water because it reminds us of the green springtime. We dip the bitter herbs in sweet charoseth to remind us that our forefathers were able to withstand bitter slavery, because it was sweetened by the hope of freedom.

CHILD: Why do we recline at the table?

LLOYD: Because reclining was a sign of a free man long ago, and since our forefathers were freed on this night, we recline at the table.

JUDITH: And so, we who are believers in Messiah can rejoice that we can keep the Passover in the days of our Messiah Yeshua. We can rejoice that in His death we have found life. In Messiah's coming the Passover was completed.

LLOYD: THE TEN PLAGUES (Exodus 7:14 through 12:29):

The Ten Plagues came about because Pharaoh would not let the children of Israel go into the desert to worship their Creator. The Lord inflicted nine plagues upon Egypt to induce Pharaoh to let the Israelites go. Pharaoh would not let them go and started a campaign to kill the firstborn of Israel. The Lord turned everything around, and the angel of death came and slew the firstborn of Egypt as a punishment.

As I mention each one of the ten plagues, everyone at the table should dip this knife into his glass of wine or grape juice, repeat the name of the plague and deposit a drop of the liquid onto his charoseth.

Each plague that our Father our King inflicted showed His superiority over the gods of the Egyptians. These are the ten plagues, which the Most Holy, Blessed be He, brought on the Egyptians in Egypt: BLOOD, BOILS, FROGS, HAIL, VERMIN, LOCUSTS, FLIES, DARKNESS, PESTILENCE, and SLAYING THE FIRST BORN.

Maggid (The story of the Exodus):

We are now going to start reading from Exodus 12:1-14 which is part of the Seder service. As I read, Judith will be showing Messiah in this passage. (The passages are read in their entirety during the Seder service, but for purposes of expediency here I will shorten the passages to make them succinct, and Judith will show the New Covenant fulfillment.)

Our Father our King said to Moses and Aaron in Egypt, "This month is to be for you the first month, the first month of your year. Tell the whole community of Israel that on the tenth day of this month each man is to take a lamb for his family, one for each household.

If any household is too small for a whole lamb, they must share one with their nearest neighbor. You are to determine the amount of lamb needed in accordance with what each person will eat. The animals you choose must be year-old males without defect, and you may take them from the sheep or the goats.

JUDITH: Yeshua entered Jerusalem on the tenth day of Nisan and was acclaimed as Messiah. He was examined by the scribes and Pharisees who could find no fault with Him.

LLOYD: The animals you choose must be year-old males.

JUDITH: Messiah was in the prime of his life.

LLOYD: And you may take them from the sheep or the goats.

JUDITH: Messiah was taken out from among men.

LLOYD: Take care of them until the fourteenth day of the month, when all the people of the community of Israel must slaughter them at twilight.

JUDITH: Messiah died on the fourteenth day of Nisan at 3p.m. the exact time and date for the killing of the Passover lamb.

LLOYD: After the Lamb was slain, the people were to take some of the blood and put it on the sides and tops of the door frames of the houses where they ate the lambs. They would put the bowl of blood down in front of the doorway of the hut, dipped their hyssop in it, and dabbed the lintel on top and then did the same for each of the doorpost they made the outline of a cross.

JUDITH: Our Creator, could have told the people to do anything He wanted them to do with the blood. Instead of telling them just to throw it against the side of the building, he used the sign of the Cross. When the angel of death passed over the huts in Egypt that fateful night, he did not strike down the firstborn of those people who were protected by the sign of the Cross.

LLOYD: "That same night you are to eat the meat roasted over the fire, along with bitter herbs and bread made without yeast. Do not eat the meat raw or cooked in water but roast it over the fire-head, legs, and inner parts. Do not leave any of it till morning; if some is left till morning, you must burn it."

JUDITH: "Messiah veiled His deity to become a man, and then He gave up His humanity on the Cross to become the perfect once-for-all sin sacrifice. Just as the Passover lamb was to be totally consumed, Yeshua gave up everything for us. He gave up His fellowship in heaven with the Father and the Spirit, a fellowship that had never been broken until the Cross. Messiah went silently to the tree; through all the beatings He did not utter a word. But on the Cross, He cries out in the agony of broken fellowship, 'My G-d my G-d, why have you forsaken me?' In Psalm 22, Yeshua answers His own question. Our Creator is holy and cannot look upon sin. Messiah, the Father's Lamb truly gave up everything."

LLOYD: "On that same night I will pass through Egypt and strike down every firstborn; both men and animals, and I will bring judgment on all the gods of Egypt. I am the L-rd. The blood will be a sign for you on the houses where you are; and when I see the blood, I will pass over you. No destructive plague will touch you when I strike Egypt. This is a day you are to commemorate. For the generations to come you shall celebrate it as a festival to Messiah, a lasting ordinance forever" (Ex. 12:14).

The L-rd our G-d has done so much for us; any one of His gifts or saving acts would have been sufficient to evoke thanks and praise from our hearts. How much then are we indebted for the manifold favors our Creator has conferred on us?

Hallel (Psalms 113 and 114):

LEADER: Praise the L-rd our G-d. All who are His servants praise His name forever.

ALL THE PEOPLE: "Let the name of the L-rd our G-d be praised both now and forever more.

LEADER: From the rising of the sun to the place where it sets, the name of our G-d is to be praised.

All THE PEOPLE: Our L-rd is exalted over all the nations, His glory above the heavens. Who is like unto our G-d the one who sits enthroned on high, who stoops down to look at things on the heavens and the earth!

LEADER: He raises the poor from the dust, and lifts the needy from the ash heap; He seats them with princes, even the princes of his people."

ALL THE PEOPLE: He settles the barren women in her home as a happy mother of children. Praise Him forever!

LEADER: When Israel came out of Egypt, the house of Jacob from people of a foreign tongue; Judah became our Father's sanctuary, Israel his dominion.

ALL THE PEOPLE: The sea looked and fled, the Jordan turned back; the mountains skipped like rams, the hills like lambs. Why was it O sea that you fled, 0 Jordan, that you turned back, you mountains, that you skipped like a rams, you hills, like lambs?

LEADER: Tremble, O earth, at the presence of the L-rd our G-d, at the presence of the Creator of Jacob, who turned the rock into a pool, the hard rock into springs of water.

THE PASCAL LAMB:

LLOYD: What was the reason our forefathers ate the Pascal lamb in Temple times? Because the Holy One, blessed be He, spared the houses of our ancestors in Egypt. In the Haggadah, it is written: "Ye shall declare, this is the Passover offering unto the L-rd our G-d who passed over the houses of the children of Israel when He struck Egypt and spared our houses. Then the people bowed in worship."

JUDITH: The Holy Scriptures say: "He was oppressed, and He was afflicted, yet He opened not His mouth: He is brought as a lamb to the slaughter, and as a sheep before her shearers is dumb, so He opened not His mouth" Isaiah 53:7. We see the fulfillment in Yeshua: "The next day John saw Yeshua coming toward him, and said, 'Behold! The Lamb of G-d who takes away the sin of the world!" John1:29.

At this point in the service the leader lifts up the plate of matzo and says the following:

LLOYD: This matzo that we eat, what is the reason for it? It is because there was not enough time for our fathers' dough to rise when the King of all Kings appeared, when the Holy and Blessed One redeemed them. The Scriptures say: "... they baked cakes of unleavened bread. The dough was without yeast because they had been driven out of Egypt and did not have time to prepare food for themselves" (Exodus 12:39).

JUDITH: Look at the matzo that is before you. You will see that the matzo is unleavened; in its baking it is pierced, bruised, and striped. It is unleavened, because it is to be without contamination. Leaven is a symbol of the meaning of sin. Pierced and striped, it illustrates the beautiful symbol of our Messiah, who, being without sin, was pierced and beaten, according to the Scripture.

In Zechariah 12:10 we read: "And I will pour out on the house of David and the inhabitants of Jerusalem a spirit of grace and supplication. They will look on Me, the one they have pierced, and they will mourn for Him as one mourns for an only child, and grieve bitterly for Him as one grieves for a firstborn son."

In Psalm 22:16 we find: "Dogs have surrounded me; a band of evil men has encircled me, they have pierced my hands and my feet". The prophet Isaiah declares in Isaiah 53:5: "But He was pierced for our transgressions, He was crushed for our iniquities; the punishment that brought us peace was upon Him and by His wounds we are healed."

LLOYD: In every generation let each man look on himself as if he came forth out of Egypt. As the Bible says, "On that day tell your son, 'I do this because of what the L-rd did for me when I came out of Egypt'" (Exod. 13:8).

It was not only our fathers that the Holy One, blessed be He, redeemed; but He redeemed us as well. The Scriptures say in Deuteronomy 6:23, 'But He brought us out from there to bring us in and give us the land that He promised on oath to our forefathers."

JUDITH: Likewise, those of us who by faith have experienced the new birth have experienced our Creator's Passover. We have been redeemed from the bondage of sin and have been placed in the heavenly realms with Messiah our bridegroom (Eph. 2:6). We are a new creation; old things have passed away; behold all things have become new (2 Cor. 5:17). Romans 6:11 tells us: "In the same way, count yourselves dead to sin but alive to G-d in Messiah Yeshua."

At this point in the service the leader raises the second cup of wine and says the following:

LLOYD: We therefore are privileged to thank, praise, adore, glorify, extol, honor, bless, exalt, and reverence Him, Who wrought all the miracles for our ancestors and us: for He brought us forth from bondage to freedom, from sorrow to joy, from mourning into holy days, from darkness to great light, and from servitude to redemption; therefore, let us chant unto him a new song, Hallelujah!

JUDITH: Truly, we can say "Hallelujah" for the great redemption which our Creator has wrought on our behalf, redemption at a terrific price. In Egypt our ancestors were redeemed from the Death of the Firstborn. As believers in Messiah Yeshua we are redeemed from the curse of sin because of the sacrifice of G-d's one and only Son. "For the L-rd so loved the world that He gave His one and only Son, that whoever believes in Him shall not perish but have eternal life" (John 3:16).

LLOYD: The drinking of the second cup is the cup of judgment, representing the second "I Will": I will rid you out of their bondage.

JUDITH: In Romans 6:15-18 we read: "What then? Shall we sin because we are not under law but under grace? By no means! Don't you know that when you offer yourselves to someone to obey him as slaves, you are slaves to the one whom you obey-whether you are slaves to sin, which leads to death, or to obedience, which leads to righteousness? But thanks be to our G-d, that though you used to be slaves to sin, you wholeheartedly obeyed the form of teaching to which you were entrusted. You have been set free from sin and have become slaves to righteousness."

At this point, before drinking from the cup for a second time, the leader raises the cup and everyone says the following blessing:

ALL: Blessed art thou, O L-rd Our G-d, King of the Universe, creator of the fruit of the vine.

MOROR (eating of the bitter herbs):

LLOYD: The leader breaks a piece of matzo from the full sheet, puts horseradish on it and gives a piece to everyone at the table. After the blessing is said, everyone will eat the Moror together. "Blessed Art thou,

O L-rd our G-d, King of the Universe, who sanctified us with His commandments and commanded us concerning the eating of bitter herbs." The bitter herb speaks of the sorrow, the persecution and the suffering of our people under the hand of Pharaoh; just as the horseradish brings tears to our eyes, so also did the great affliction of our people bring tears to their eyes.

KOREKH (eating of the bitter herbs with the sweet Charoseth):

The leader of the Seder breaks two pieces from the bottom matzo in the unity bag for every person at the table. He puts Charoseth on one piece and horseradish on the other piece. They are then put together to make a sandwich. When this is done everyone eats this sandwich together.

LLOYD: As the bitter herb is a symbol of suffering, the salt water a symbol of tears, the greens a symbol of hyssop, and the wine a symbol of blood, so the Charoseth is a symbol of mortar, representing the clay bricks that were made by our people in Egypt.

JUDITH: Concerning this mixture of the bitter and the sweet-we read in John 13:25-27: "Leaning back against Jesus (Yeshua), he asked Him, 'Lord who is it?' Yeshua answered 'It is the one to whom I will give this piece of bread when I have dipped in the dish.' Then, dipping the piece of bread, He gave it to Judas Iscariot, son of Simon. As soon as Judas took the bread, Satan entered into him."

This is the sop which Messiah gave to Judas. The symbolism of the bitter and the sweet is seen in the bitterness of His betrayal by a friend and the sweetness of the redemption He provided for all those who would come to Him for salvation.

At this point, the service is suspended while the food is brought to the table so everyone can eat the Passover meal together. While the food is being brought to the table, the children will look for the middle piece of matzo that was broken at the beginning of the service and wrapped in a linen napkin and hidden by the leader. When the children find it they will take this piece of matzo that is called the Afikomen and hold that for a ransom.

When the supper is over the service continues.

TZAPHUN (eating of the Afikomen):

LLOYD: The Afikomen is our substitute for the Paschal Lamb, which in days of old, was the final food of the Seder Feast. Before the service can continue the leader must buy back the Afikomen from the children who have searched for and found it. The Matzo is broken and distributed, in olive size pieces, to each of the guests.

JUDITH: Concerning the Afikomen, it is written: 'And He took bread, gave thanks and broke it, and gave it to them, saying, "This is My body given for you: do this in remembrance of Me"' (Luke 22:19).

Concerning the Messiah, it is written:

> Yeshua said to them, "I tell you the truth, it is not Moses who has given you the bread from heaven, but it is my Father who gives you the true bread from heaven. For the bread of our Creator is He who comes down from heaven and gives life to the world."
>
> "Sir," they said, "from now on give us this bread." Then Messiah Yeshua declared, "I am the bread of life. He who comes to Me will never go hungry, and he who believes in Me will never be thirsty...."
>
> "I am the bread of life. Your forefathers ate the manna in the desert, yet they died. But here is the bread that comes down from heaven, which a man may eat and not die. I am the living bread that came down from heaven. If anyone eats of this bread, he will live forever. This bread is My flesh, which I will give for the life of the world…. The Spirit gives life; the flesh counts for nothing. The words I have spoken to you are spirit and they are life'" (John 6: 32-35 and 6:48-51, 63.
>
> It is highly significant that this middle matzo was broken and then hidden away. It is finally redeemed for a price. It is broken again and then distributed to those celebrating the Passover. It is this piece of matzo to which our Savior refers when He says "This is my body which is given for you."
>
> It is also significant that Afikomen means, "I have come."
>
> Remember, the matzo is unleavened, it is bruised; it is striped; and it is pierced. Even so, the Messiah was unleavened: that is, sinless. Even so, the Messiah was bruised by the rod and by their fists. Even

so, Messiah was given stripes by the beater. Even so, the Messiah was pierced; that is, by the nails in his hands and his feet and by the spear in his side.

If you are a believer in Messiah Yeshua, you can eat this piece as in a communion service, reminding yourself of what happened in the upper room at the Last Supper. Also, as you eat, it will remind you of what the Messiah did for you, in that He came and gave Himself for your sins.

Let us search out the leaven of sin in our lives; and so let us keep the Feast of Unleavened Bread---the Passover-as it is written: 'A man ought to examine himself before he eats of the bread and drinks of the cup'" (1 Cor. 11:28).

LLOYD: In a typical Jewish service, everyone will then eat a piece of the Afikomen. The rabbis call this the dessert because it is the last thing eaten at the Passover meal. They say that it is very important that everyone at the table eats some of it, even the smallest baby. The rabbis cannot explain the word Afikomen. It is Greek and not Hebrew. It is the only Greek word in this whole service and as Judith said before, it means "I have come". As Messianic believers, we believe that early Jewish believers inserted this into the Passover service as a sign for future generations that Messiah came and did His work of redemption. Once something becomes a tradition in Judaism, it is continued even if there is not any explanation for it.

The leader recites the following blessing:

LLOYD: Blessed art thou O L-rd our G-d, King of the universe, who brings forth bread from the earth.

Everyone at the table eats a piece of the Afikomen. Traditionally, Jewish people eat it as part of the Passover service, while those who are believers in Messiah Yeshua eat it as part of the Lord's Supper.

At this point in the service the third cup is filled and elevated.

The leader of the Seder says the following:

LLOYD: This cup represents the third "I Will": "I will redeem you." This is our Savior's promise that He would redeem His people from slavery. To the Jewish person celebrating the Passover, this is just part of the Passover service. To those of us who are reborn by the Spirit of the Almighty One, this is part of the Lord's Supper.

JUDITH: After the supper in the upper room, Messiah raised this cup and stated: "'This cup is the new covenant in my blood, which is poured out for you" (Luke 22:20). Our Messiah came, died, and shed His blood as the final Passover Lamb. He did this to provide salvation for all who would place their faith and trust in Him.

At this point in the service, the leader recites the following blessing:

LLOYD: Blessed art Thou, O L-rd our G-d, King of the Universe, who creates the fruit of the vine.

After the blessing everyone drinks the cup together.

Elijah is the unseen guest at every Passover service. There is a special place set for him at the Passover table. His place is the place of honor at the table. The leader lifts up the cup of Elijah, which has not been used up to this point, and says the following:

LLOYD: This cup is for Elijah the Prophet, ELIYAHU HANAVI.

At this time during the service, one of the children will open the door to see if Elijah is there. When he is not, everyone at the table will say that maybe next year he will come. Everyone knows Elijah must come to precede Messiah.

JUDITH: "See, I will send you the prophet Elijah before that great and dreadful day of Messiah comes" (Mal. 4:5).

LLOYD: Elijah did not see death, but was swept up to heaven by a great whirlwind, in a chariot of fire. It has been our hope that Elijah would come at Passover, to announce the Messiah, the Son of David.

JUDITH: Before the birth of John the Baptizer, an angel of the L-rd said: "And he will go on before Messiah, in the spirit and power of Elijah…to make ready a people prepared for the Creator" (Luke 1:17).

LLOYD: Later, Yeshua spoke of John.

JUDITH: "And if you are willing to accept it, he is the Elijah who was to come" (Matt. 11:14).

LLOYD: It was this same John who saw Yeshua and declared:

JUDITH: "Look, the Lamb of G-d, who takes away the sin of the world!" (John 1:29).

LLOYD: We come to the fourth and last drinking of the cup. This cup represents the fourth "I will": "I will take you to me for a people." This speaks of the time when Messiah will again gather Israel to Himself."

JUDITH: To the believer in Messiah Yeshua, this cup also represents the great hope that the Messiah is coming back to take His followers to be with Him. It is written, "For the Messiah Himself will come down from heaven, with a loud command, with the voice of the archangel and with the trumpet call of G-d, and the dead in Messiah will rise first. After that, we who are still alive and are left will be caught up together with them in the clouds to meet Messiah in the air. And so we will be with Him forever" (1 Thess. 4:16-17).

LLOYD: After the blessing is said, everyone drinks the fourth cup together. "Blessed art thou, O L-rd our G-d, King of the Universe, Creator of the fruit of the vine."

After the fourth cup, everyone knows that the Seder is ending. The father recites the following blessing:

Blessed are you, O L-rd, Our G-d, King of the Universe, for the wine, and for the fruit of the vine, and for the produce of the field and for that desirable, good and spacious land which you granted our ancestors to inherit, to eat of its fruit, and be satisfied with its goodness.

Have compassion upon us O L-rd our G-d, on Israel your people, upon Jerusalem, your city on Zion, the residence of your glory, and upon the altar and your Temple; rebuild Jerusalem, your Holy city, speedily in our days. Cheer us on this day of the Feast of Unleavened Bread, for thou, O Eternal, Our King, art good and benevolent unto all, and therefore do we thank you for the land, and for the fruit of the vine. Blessed are you, O Eternal, for the land and for the fruit of the vine.

The Seder of Passover is now complete - even as our salvation and redemption are complete. As we are privileged to celebrate it this year, so may we be privileged to do so in the future.

CONCLUSION:

Passover celebrates our Creator's deliverance of the Jewish people from slavery in Egypt. It is also a celebration by the born-again believer of the end of his slavery to sin. Just as the Israelites went to celebrate the feast of Passover, as believers in the Father of Abraham, Isaac, and Jacob (John 12:20), so should New Covenant believers celebrate the feast as the seal of their own salvation (1 Cor. 5:7b and 8). In addition, they are to celebrate the L-rd's Supper as their source of strength and vitality in their new creation.

Passover is the fulfillment of the covenant the Eternal One made with Abraham in Genesis 15:13ff and to which Exodus 12:40ff refers: "Then the L-rd said to him, 'Know for certain that your descendants will be strangers in a country not their own, and they will be enslaved and mistreated four hundred years. But I will punish the nation they serve as slaves, and afterward they will come out with great possessions. You, however, will go to your fathers in peace and be buried at a good old age. In the fourth generation your descendants will come back here, for the sin of the Amorites is not yet reached its full measure'" (Gen. 15:13ff).

Exodus 12:40ff says: "Now the length of time the Israelite people lived in Egypt was 430 years. At the end of the 430 years, all our L-rd's divisions left Egypt. Because the L-rd our G-d kept vigil that night to bring them out of Egypt, on this night all the Israelites are to keep vigil to honor their Creator for the generations to come."

The initiation of our Creator's covenant with His servant Abram is recorded in Genesis 15:7ff: "He also said to him, 'I am the L-rd, who brought you out of Ur of the Chaldeans to give you this land to take possession of it.' But Abram said, 'O Sovereign L-rd, how can I know that I will gain possession of it?' So the L-r said to him, 'Bring me a heifer, a goat and a ram, each three years old, along with a dove and a young pigeon.' Abram brought all these to Him, cut them in two and arranged the halves opposite each other; the birds, however he did not cut in half. Then birds of prey came down on the carcasses, but Abram drove them away. As the sun was setting, Abram fell into a deep sleep, and a thick and dreadful darkness came over him."

Verses 17 through 21 complete the account: "When the sun had set and darkness had fallen, a smoking firepot with a blazing torch appeared and passed between the pieces. On that day the L-rd made a covenant with Abram and said, 'To your descendants I give this land, from the river of Egypt to the great river, the Euphrates-the land of the Kenites, Kenizzites, Kadmonites, Hittites, Perizzites, Rephaites, Amorites, Canaanites, Girgashites, and Jebusites.'"

Abram prepared the sacrifice, and then the L-rd put him into a deep sleep. While Abram was in that deep sleep, the L-rd made a covenant with him and through him with his posterity. The L-rd alone walked through the midst of the animal parts, showing that this was a one-sided covenant in which the L-rd did all the work. The L-rd our G-d was the initiator, accomplisher, and finisher; and Abram was the receiver. This meant that the covenant was unconditional and unilateral.

In Jeremiah 31:31ff, we read of another unilateral covenant. It is the New Covenant given by the L-rd our G-d for the redemption of all those sinners that would be given to Messiah Yeshua for salvation. This covenant was also unconditional. It was unilaterally made by our Father and guaranteed unconditional election to all those who the Father gave to Messiah Yeshua. The temporal physical salvation of the Jewish people at Passover was a type of the spiritual permanent salvation that was provided by Messiah Yeshua because of His sacrifice on the Cross at Calvary.

The concept of a sacrificial type is demonstrated in more than just the Passover. The burnt offering, required by the Levitical legal system, was a free-will offering by the Israelites unto their L-rd. It was an offering, made by fire, which was a sweet-smelling savor unto the L-rd. The sinner who made the offering put his hands upon the animal to be sacrificed and symbolically transferred his sin to the animal. This was required under the law, even though it did not take away sin. It covered sin only until the time of the New Covenant, when sin would be taken away by the sacrifice of Messiah. The fact that the sacrifices had to be constantly repeated year after year showed that the offeror was never made clean before his Creator. After Messiah was sacrificed, He sat down at the right hand of the Father because His sacrifice was efficacious for all who would come to Him (Heb 10:1-12). Neither the highest ecclesiastical authority (the Sanhedrin) nor the highest civil authority (the Roman governor), could find fault in Yeshua. He was the perfect sacrifice required by our heavenly Father for the payment of all the sins of all His people. The L-rd our G-d said, "This is my beloved Son, in whom I am well pleased" (Matt.17:5b). We who are reborn by the spirit of G-d are in Messiah. Because we are in Messiah, our heavenly Father is well pleased with us also.

In the covenant with Abram, we notice further symbolism. There were three large animals, each three years old. The number three in Scripture speaks of majesty, as in the Triune Majesty. The Royal Majesty of the Godhead doubly confirms a covenant in which it does all the work. To eliminate any possible confusion as to the people with whom the covenant was made, our L-rd used two birds. They were not cut up, but were left whole. This signified that the receivers of the covenant, as represented by Abram, were two totally distinct people. The typology is that those who would receive salvation would come from two separate peoples, the Jews and the Gentiles.

The L-rd our G-d created mankind in glory and placed him in the Garden of Eden. Mankind fell (through his own disobedience) from that glory. Adam's disobedience resulted in condemnation for all men. Both of the covenants that our Creator made with Abraham (in Genesis 12 and 15) were to be completed by Messiah, so that just as there was disobedience unto dishonor by one man, there would be obedience unto glory by another man (Romans 5:12). In Abraham's seed all peoples on earth were to be blessed. It was a foregone conclusion that the second Adam could not and would not fail to return glory to the Godhead. To accomplish this, Messiah submitted Himself to the Godhead and became incarnate as a human being. He would satisfy all the requirements that would be needed to bring a redeemed people as His personal body and bride to an eternal state in Heaven.

Paul writes in Ephesians 1:3-9 that the Father of our Messiah has blessed us in heavenly realms with every spiritual blessing, for He chose us in Him before the creation of the world to be holy and blameless in His sight. He predestinated us to be adopted as His sons through Yeshua the Messiah, in accordance with His pleasure and will---to the praise of His glorious grace, which He has freely given us in the one He loves. In Him, we have redemption through His blood, the forgiveness of sins, in accordance with the riches of our Father's grace.

Just as the blood on the huts of the Jewish people in Egypt gave them salvation from death in the natural sense, the blood of Messiah spilled upon the cross at Calvary gives all believers salvation in the spiritual sense. The covenants with Abraham look forward to the vindication of our Father's creation. Unregenerate men are blind to the path of redemption. They are totally unaware that their actions are in direct opposition to our Creator's precepts.

The natural, physical promises of the Abrahamic covenant have a corresponding spiritual fulfillment. The Jewish people are in the natural lineage of Abraham, while the body of Messiah is in the spiritual lineage of Abraham (Gal. 3:7-9). Therefore, the physical land that is described is for Israel (the Jewish people) in the natural lineage in the natural sense. Natural salvation for the natural lineage of Abraham came at Passover. Spiritual salvation for Abraham's spiritual descendants came at Calvary when they (both Jews and Gentiles) became the body and bride of Messiah as well as a kingdom of priests (1 Pet. 2:9). Those who are spiritual descendants of Abraham have spiritual redemption and a spiritual land promise also. They are a new creation; old things have passed away; behold all things have become new (2 Cor. 5:17). Thus, while believers are residents on this earth, they are also seated in the heavenlies with Messiah (Eph. 2:6-10). Messiah has been and now is preparing a place for all believers who are now seated in His kingdom by faith (John 14:2-3).

By faith Abraham made his home in the Promised Land. Like a stranger in a foreign country, he lived in tents, as did Isaac and Jacob, who were heirs with him of the same promise. They were looking forward to the city with foundations, whose architect and builder is G-d. They admitted that they were aliens and strangers on earth. They were longing for a better country—a heavenly one (Heb. 11). They entered the eternal kingdom by faith in the One they never saw. The patriarchs, as well as many Jewish and Gentile people who exhibited faith before the time of Messiah on this earth, will be there.

Many of Abraham's natural lineage stumbled at the stumbling stone. They replaced faith in their Creator with works of their hands. The Scriptures teach clearly that national ancestry is not the same as spiritual ancestry. Along with our father Abraham, we believers are strangers and sojourners upon this earth. We, along with him, look for the city that is presently our spiritual home, where we will spend eternity. It is the city whose builder and maker is the King of Kings and L-rd of L-rd's. (Hebrews 11).

It is a privilege to celebrate the Passover and to be reminded that physical salvation is not the same thing as spiritual salvation. Even though our Creator provided physical salvation for the people in Egypt, they later rebuffed His commands and did not enter into His eternal rest. This is verified by the fact that our Creator said (of the generation that was the proper age in Egypt and came out to the promised land) that only a certain few would enter His rest. While we celebrate this holiday in the physical sense, in a much greater sense we are celebrating it spiritually. Messiah our Passover Lamb has been sacrificed. Therefore let us keep the festival, not with the old yeast of malice and wickedness, but with bread without yeast, the bread of sincerity and truth (1 Cor. 5:7b and 8).

This is what I am suggesting to all believers: celebrate all the feasts in the fullness of Messiah Yeshua. By doing so, you will fulfill Romans 11:11b. You will make the Jewish people jealous of your celebration of a holiday they consider their own. As the L-rd our G-d uses this jealousy to bring them to Himself, you will be fulfilling Isaiah 49:22. If the Holy Spirit uses you to be a witness to lost Israel, then our Creator gets the glory. Do all things for His glory. DO NOT celebrate Passover or any of the feasts for the sake of merely celebrating them. It does not matter if you celebrate them in the rabbinic tradition or the Messianic tradition; both are equally invalid. Neither recognizes that all the feasts are fulfilled by the work of Yeshua the Messiah. DO NOT DO IT; JUST DO NOT DO IT! If any of the Levitical feasts are still unfulfilled, then the Old Covenant is not completely closed (Heb. 8 and Gal. 4). The only way to celebrate the feasts is as a wife, preparing a banquet feast for her victorious husband who is King of Kings and L-rd of L-rd's our glorious Creator. All by Himself, He has accomplished all that was needed for the salvation of every believer. Give the glory to Him to whom all glory is due.

The Feast of Unleavened Bread

INTRODUCTION

Leviticus 23 introduces the Feast of Unleavened Bread, along with the institution of the Passover. It is quite common to confuse the two, and many people use the terms interchangeably. The misunderstanding comes from Luke 22:1 which reads, "Now the Feast of Unleavened Bread, called the Passover, was approaching". Actually, they are two separate celebrations; the single-day feast, Passover, is celebrated on the first evening of the first day of a week-long festival, the Feast of Unleavened Bread. In Israel's calendar a specific day began from what we would call the night before. This coincides with our Creator's accounting in the days of creation. The evening and the morning made up the day. A day was counted from sunset of one day to sunset of the following day. Passover was observed on the evening of the 15th (the beginning of the 15th in the Jewish calendar, but the end of the 14th in our calendar) of the month of Nisan, and the convocation of the Feast of Unleavened Bread was celebrated from the evening of the 15th through the evening of 21st.

In Deuteronomy 16:3, while referring to the celebration of the Passover and the killing of the lamb, the L-rd our G-d gives the following instructions: "Do not eat it [the lamb] with bread made with yeast, but for seven days eat unleavened bread, the bread of affliction…" Why does the L-rd our G-d refer to the bread as "the bread of affliction"? Some people say that the nature of unleavened bread makes it an affliction to eat. It is curious, but I never knew anyone who thought it was an affliction to eat matzo during the Feast of Unleavened Bread. After all, we put all kinds of food on the matzo. I have covered it with chopped liver, chicken salad, peanut butter and jelly, lox and cream cheese and on and on. It was definitely not a burden to eat matzo for one week.

I would submit to you that there are three aspects to consider in this description of the bread of affliction. One of the reasons for its designation is found in the passage in Deuteronomy: "…because you left Egypt in haste-so that all the days of your life you may remember the time of your departure from Egypt" (Deut. 16:3b). The Israelites' hasty departure from Egypt was the result of our L-rd's deliverance of them from the slavery and oppression they experienced there. The L-rd our G-d had heard their groaning and taken pity on their affliction, in accordance with His covenant with Abraham (Gen. 15:12-14). Their entire experience as slaves in Egypt was an affliction. In this manner, the bread of affliction serves as a reminder of our Father's faithfulness to His promise in a purely physical sense. Our Father's regenerate people may also apply the concept as a metaphor for the affliction of slavery to sin. In this manner, the bread of affliction serves as a reminder that our Father is faithful in a spiritual sense to His promise to Adam to destroy (crush) the serpent's head (Gen. 3:15) and to deliver those who all their lives were held in slavery by their fear of death (Heb. 2:15). Ultimately, though, this has a typological aspect. Our Father called this the bread of affliction because he looked forward to the time when Messiah Yeshua would be sacrificed on Calvary's cross. This bread anticipated the bread Messiah gave to his disciples and said, "Take and eat; this is my body that was given for you" (Matt. 26:26 with Luke 22:19). His body had striped and was bruised by the whip; it was also broken for the redeemed (1 Cor. 11:24). I believe that this is the ultimate reason for the unleavened bread being called the bread of affliction.

THREE QUESTIONS AND THEIR ANSWERS

How was the Feast of Unleavened Bread established?

How was and is the Feast of Unleavened Bread celebrated?

What are the implications of the Feast of Unleavened Bread under the New Covenant?

How was the Feast of Unleavened Bread established?

The Holy Scriptures record the establishment of this convocation in Exodus 12:15-20, Leviticus 23:6-8, and Numbers 28:17-25. "On the fifteenth day of that month our Creator's Feast of Unleavened Bread begins; for seven days you must eat bread without yeast. On the first day hold a sacred assembly and do no regular work. For seven days present an offering made to our Father by fire. And on the seventh day hold a sacred assembly and do no regular work" (Lev. 23:6-8).

Deuteronomy 16:3 ff. tells us that the Feast of Unleavened Bread along with the Feast of Passover was to be celebrated as a remembrance of Israel's departure from Egypt.

The Feast of Unleavened Bread

How was and is the Feast of Unleavened Bread celebrated?

There was only one original Feast of Unleavened Bread. From that point on, every time the children of Israel celebrated this Feast, it was celebrated as a memorial to what the children of Israel did when they departed from Egypt.

Historically, the children of Israel were very scrupulous in its observance. Even today they use this holiday as a rallying point to show the sovereignty of our Father in this world. The Jewish people were very careful to remove leaven from their homes. In addition, the Scripture says they were not to work during this period. The only work they were allowed to do was relative to their getting food to eat.

Not only was Israel required to abstain from eating leaven, but she also was required to remove leaven from all her habitations. This put great pressure on the woman of the house. Since yeast is airborne, everything in the house had to be cleaned. Actually, the job of removing leaven from the home was much easier when houses were constructed and furnished in a simpler manner than that of today.

People in ancient times made bread with a starter. This starter was a small lump of dough that had risen on a previous occasion. When the housewife wanted to make bread, she would take this starter and add it to the flour and water mixture that she was going to use to make the bread. When the whole batch had risen, she would take a piece out of it, wrap it up, and put it in a moist place. This became the starter for the next batch of bread. The next time she wanted to bake bread, she would follow the same procedure.

In ancient days, the Israelites understood the separation from leaven. They understood that if they had leaven in their houses during the Feast of Unleavened Bread, they would be cut off from Israel. When it was time for the Feast, a housewife could no longer keep her starter mixture. She had to destroy it. After the Feast of Unleavened Bread, she would have to put her flour and water mixture outside to wait for airborne yeast to land on it and cause it to rise. At that point, she would again have her starter to use to bake bread throughout the year. A traditional and very welcome gift for a new bride would be a batch of starter so that she could immediately start to bake bread.

Over the centuries, an elaborate ritual has developed for the removal of leaven from a home. During a given period before the day of preparation and on the day of preparation, the house is thoroughly cleaned. The floors, walls, and ceilings are scrubbed; pots and utensils are scoured and boiled. Some homes have special dishes that are brought out for the Feast of Unleavened Bread and then put away when the Festival is over. Other homes that do not have special dishes wash their regular dishes in extra-hot water to kill all the leaven.

The mother will hide some leaven at different places in the house. When the father comes home from prayers at the Synagogue, he searches for the leaven. Reminiscent of the days before there was electricity, the father will take a candle, wooden spoon, and feather to search for the leaven. As the father searches for the leaven, those who hid it will tell him when he is warmer or colder until he finds all the leaven. Once all the leaven is found, the father uses the feather to brush it on to the wooden spoon and then puts all leaven together and burns it so it is destroyed. When that is done, he will say a prayer and pronounce the house free of contamination and fit to celebrate the Passover.

All of this occurs before 3:00 p.m. on the day of preparation for the Passover. In ancient times, the Passover sacrifice was killed by 3:00 in the afternoon. Even though the Passover service in the home would not start until after sundown, the house had to be cleaned and ready to celebrate the Passover by the time the Passover sacrifice would be killed.

The Scriptures constantly equate leaven with sin, and only those who are truly reborn of the Spirit have the ability to detect sin's subtleties. When the New Testament writers spoke about the relationship between leaven and sin, their audience knew exactly what they were talking about. The leaven, or sin and wickedness, did not exist in isolation. It was not a onetime occurrence. Just as in the case of the starter, in which the leaven from the first batch of dough permeated every subsequent batch of dough until it was finally destroyed before the Feast of Unleavened Bread, so do sin and wickedness go on and on in a person's lifetime. Just as there was a time when the leaven in a Jewish person's home had to be destroyed, so there would come a time when sin and wickedness on this earth would be vanquished by Messiah Yeshua.

The Pharisees had always put a tremendous emphasis on the oral law. The oral law was codified as the Talmud in approximately 300 A.D. The oral law tells us in Berachot 17 that leaven was a representative of the evil impulse of the heart. The Jewish people could personally identify with the fact that a little leaven (sin and wickedness) could infect a much larger group or lump, as the Scripture says.

Exodus 13:9 describes another important part of the Feast of Unleavened Bread, "It shall be as a sign to you on your hand and as a memorial between your eyes that the L-ord's law may be in your mouth; for with a strong hand our L-rd has brought us out of Egypt. You shall therefore keep this ordinance in its season from year to year."

Historically, Jewish people observed this command by the development of phylacteries. In religious homes, when a male reaches thirteen years of age, he is considered to be an adult and is counted in the formation of a prayer group. It is at this time that he is given his own set of phylacteries. These are small leather prayer cases that consist of two separate cubes. Each of the cubes has two leather straps that pass through hollow extensions that protrude from the back of the cases. In each one of the boxes there are Scripture verses. One part of the set is tied around the head and the other part of the set is wrapped around the left arm and the fingers of the left hand. The wearing of the phylacteries was intended to be an aid in remembering the events and instruction recorded in Scripture, as well as an aid to stress sanctity of mind in order to prevent levity when involved in prayer or devotion before our holy Father. Some Orthodox Jewish men tie on their phylacteries when they pray; but it is safe to say that most Jewish men do not. This external act does not make someone godlier or more acceptable to our holy Father. Man looks on the outside, but the L-rd G-d looks on the heart (I Samuel 16:7) Too often, the physical act that was to signify a heart attitude has replaced the attitude and become itself the more important matter. It becomes habit. The wearing of phylacteries by modern Jewish men is just one example of an external act that can be completely divorced from any heart attitude of love for our Creator.

I submit to you that we should look at this verse in a spiritual sense. Messianic Jews believe that the observance of the Feast of Unleavened Bread is to be spiritualized to apply to everything people do with their hands, everything they see with their eyes, and everything they say with their mouths. The leaven of sin is to be removed from every area of life- body, mind, heart, and will. It is for all day, every day of their lives, and not just for specific, limited periods of time. It was and is designed to make a holy people. Not only must the words of our mouth, but also the meditations of our hearts be acceptable to the Holy One praise be His name.

We should remember that this Feast was a celebration in two parts. Not only were the Israelites required to remember what their Father had done for them and pass it on to their children, but they also had to do the work of not eating bread with leaven in it. Their remembrance was consecrated by their actions. The seven-day period of this Feast was a time of separation from worldly endeavors to reflect on the things of their Father. The people were reminded of their Father's presence by what they did not eat, as well as by the fact that they did no regular labor.

Natural Israel assumed that the physical observance of the written word is the same as the spiritual observance of the written word. She falsely assumed that, because she had natural lineage from the patriarchs, she also had spiritual lineage from the patriarchs. Nothing could be further from the truth. Israel stumbled at the stumbling stone time after time and continues to do so as a nation even to this day. She is not alone in this error. Many of those who say they are Christians and followers of the Jewish Messiah today have made the exact same mistake. They stumble at the stumbling stone. They assume that an outward profession of faith is the same as an inward possession of the Spirit. They assume that, because they have parents or grandparents who are believers inheriting eternal salvation, they also are automatically believers who will inherit eternal salvation. They make an outward profession, but they are devoid of an inward possession of their Creator's Spirit. Nothing could be further from the truth this false confidence is a device of the devil.

What are the implications of the Feast of Unleavened Bread under the New Covenant?

For those with spiritual eyes, the Feast of Unleavened Bread speaks of the spiritual creation, a creation that is quite different from everything around them. Although they still dwell in the natural realm, the Feast of Unleavened Bread raises them to the spiritual realm. This Feast has them partake of normal unleavened bread that is the spiritual food that Yeshua the Messiah gave them. When, as Messianic believers, they celebrate this convocation, their celebration is in the spiritual creation, as well as in the natural creation.

Under the New Covenant, the spiritual implications of this convocation are astounding. The Israelites were to separate themselves physically from what was their normal daily routine. If they did not, they were to be cut off from their people. Those who are reborn of the Spirit and are a new creation in Messiah Yeshua must mentally and spiritually separate themselves from the world in which they exist. We are part of this world, put here to be salt and light; but we are not to adopt the values and attitudes that characterize the world.

If you know some people who say they are reborn by the Spirit of the L-rd G-d and nothing has changed from the way they were before their profession, you have the right to wonder if anything supernatural ever happened to them. A person may say that he has faith, but he might have no works as evidence of that faith. The Scripture tells us "faith without works is dead." Dead faith is no faith.

True believers are a new creation; old things have passed away; behold all things have become new (2 Cor. 5:17). The person who is born again by the Spirit of our Father has a great responsibility and motivation to tell others what our Father has done for him. He is a new believer in the spiritual creation. The precepts of our L-rd and G-d are to be constantly before this believer when he looks out of his eyes, when he speaks with his mouth, and when he uses his hands. The work of our hands is to be Messiah's work. Our standard is not just an earthly standard; it is the heavenly standard given to us by Messiah. This standard is not only for the words of our mouths and the works of our hands, but it must be applied also to the meditations of our hearts. Messiah is not only our Passover Lamb; He is also our unleavened bread. He is the bread of sincerity and truth.

When He gave us His supper, and said, "take, eat, this is my body," He was giving us His body of sinlessness. He came down from Heaven without any sin, and remained sinless while He was on this earth. That is precisely why He is the kinsman-redeemer to all who come to Him for salvation.

The strength of a believer comes from the Spirit of Messiah, as well as from the partaking of the elements of Messiah's Supper. We are His bride, and as such it behooves us to strive to be more like Him. Just as He despises sin, so also we are to despise it. Our glorying is to be in Him, and not in the things of this world.

Israel was to remember her exodus from Egypt and glorify her L-rd and her G-d for His redemption. She did that once a year. We as believers are to remember our spiritual salvation and give constant glory to our Father daily, on a moment by moment basis, and not just on an annual basis.

Johanan ben Zakkai is considered to be the father of Rabbinic Judaism. He taught salvation without the necessary requirement of blood. The Talmud tells us that he spent the first forty years of his life in business, the second forty years of his life studying, and the last forty years of his life ministering to the people. It is said, to his credit, that he would not walk more than a few feet without meditating on the law of his Creator. Now I ask you, if this man, who did not receive spiritual salvation, could meditate on his Creator's law at such regular intervals, what greater ability and motivation must fill someone who has been reborn by our Creator's Spirit?

Just as Israel was set free from Egypt, which was her house of bondage, those of us who are one with Messiah have been removed from the house of bondage of this world. Old things have passed away; behold all things have become new. We are not sinless and never will be while we reside on this earth, but we must constantly press toward the mark for the high calling of our Father in Messiah Yeshua.

The Israelites were required to purge their house of leaven, once a year, before they celebrated the Feast of Unleavened Bread. Under the New Covenant believers are encouraged to do this daily. We are told: "Know ye not [it is a foregone conclusion] that a little leaven leaveneth the whole lump? Purge out therefore the old leaven, that ye may be a new lump, as you are unleavened" (1 Cor.5:6b-7a) . Believers must be involved in a constant process of renewal, a constant "re-attaching" of themselves to Messiah. "For even Christ [Messiah] our passover is sacrificed for us: Therefore let us keep the feast, not with old leaven, neither with the leaven of malice and wickedness; but with the unleavened bread of sincerity and truth" (1st Cor. 5:7b-8, [KJV]). As we gaze lovingly at the Savior of our souls and meditate on all His perfections as they are recorded in Scripture and revealed to us by the Holy Spirit, we will be changed to become more like Him (2 Cor. 3:12-18). This is a never-ending process until the day we reside in completeness with Messiah in His eternal Kingdom.

Just as Israel was to show her sons what her L-rd had done for her, we as believers are to show our children what He has done for us. We are to teach them His Scriptures, for they contain the secrets of eternal life the truth about Messiah. We are to teach our children the Holy Scriptures when they sit down, when they rise up, and when they walk by the way. When we do this, the world may say that we are not flexible, that we are too rigid, and that we deprive our children of experiencing true life. Those who are true believers know that the world must be behind us while the cross must be before us.

Those of us who have our Heavenly Father's law in our heart should also give Him the praise of our lips so that at all times we may give Him glory for His salvation. We who are believers are to be a holy people separated unto the L-rd our G-d who is our King . The purging out of the leaven of sin in our lives is supposed to be something that is aggressive and not passive. As believers, we are not to see how close we can get to sin; but in reality we are to stay as far away from sin as we can. Does our light so shine that those around us know that we are different? Can they see that we strive to be more like the One we call our Lord and Savior? If people cannot tell us apart from the world, our testimony for Messiah is deficient. We are to leave the leaven of this world behind and strive toward righteousness, holiness, and truth. Let us, as born-again believers, be as conscientious about removing leaven from our lives as the religious Jewish person was about removing leaven from his house during this convocation. Who knows what the outcome would be? It would be wonderful if it resulted in the whole world being turned upside down to the glory of Messiah!

II Corinthians 6:17, 18 tells us, "Wherefore (because of our Creator's promise to dwell in His people and to be their G-d, and they His people) come out from among them, and be separate, saith the L-rd, and touch not the unclean thing; and I will receive you, and will be a Father unto you, and ye shall be my sons and daughters, saith the L-rd Almighty". If your testimony to the world around you is not what it should be or is not what you would like it to be, ask our Father to help you. He will show you great and mighty things to do to give Him glory.

CONCLUSION:

We celebrate this convocation to show our Father's faithfulness and as a reminder that we are to resist evil and seek righteousness.

Let us look back at the Exodus for a moment. Once Israel was through the Red Sea, she was safe from the pursuing Egyptians. She received physical salvation as a nation, but not all received spiritual salvation. The angel of death passed over their huts in Egypt when he saw the markings of the bloody cross on their lintels and doorposts. We who are reborn by the Spirit of G-d do not have blood on our lintels and doorposts. In reality, we are covered by the blood and righteousness of Yeshua the Messiah. That covering is our wedding garment. It is that garment that makes us fit to be the bride of Messiah. As the bride of Messiah, we are to strive constantly to purge out the leaven of sin in us so that we may be made a new lump, which means that we will be made more conformed to His image.

Messiah is our Passover and has been sacrificed for us; therefore, let us keep the feast, not with the old leaven, neither with the leaven of malice and wickedness, but with the unleavened bread of sincerity and truth. As believers, the pursuit of godliness is to be constantly before us. We are to do acts of His mercy and then tell others about His salvation. The Feast of Unleavened Bread was celebrated for seven days. Seven is the number of completion in the Scriptures. Even though we will never attain that perfection in this life, we are to press constantly toward the mark for the high calling in Messiah Yeshua.

It is worth repeating again – we who are believers are to refrain from sin and constantly seek the face of Messiah, not just for one week out of the year but for each and every day of our lives. Even though we constantly fall short of the glory of the L-rd, we must constantly press toward the mark of His high calling. (Ephesians 2:6) It is important to remember that we can do all things through Messiah who strengthens us. There is no temptation that can totally overcome those who are reborn of the Spirit, because greater is He that is in us than He that is in the world. (I John 4:4) We must always flee to Messiah for daily cleansing from sin.

Believers need to preach the gospel to themselves, to be reminded that Messiah has paid for all their sin, too. Since it has already been removed as far as the East is from the West, we can live in that reality. Messiah Yeshua is stronger and more powerful than we, and He acts on our behalf in sanctification as well as justification.

For over nineteen-hundred years many people who have said that they were Christians and followers of the Jewish Messiah persecuted and abused the Jewish people. The Jewish people were beaten, raped, and murdered; they had their children and property taken away from them in the name of Christ. It is ludicrous to think that those people who abused the Jewish people in the name of the Jewish Messiah will get into Heaven. They have had their reward for their deeds on this earth. The Scripture tells us that we are known by our fruit. Their fruit is not the fruit of righteousness, but it is the fruit of their father the devil. They will be judged by the judgment they used and their account will be found wanting in righteousness.

Our example is Yeshua the Messiah. Isaiah 53:9 tells us, "He had done no violence, neither was any deceit in his mouth." John 8:46 tells us that no one could prove Him guilty of sin. Pilate said that he found no fault in Messiah. Neither the civil authority nor the ecclesiastical authority could ethically condemn Him. He is the only one who could accomplish salvation for all those whom His Father would give Him, because He was the only one on this earth who never sinned. The testimony of Messiah Himself is pure and undefiled even to this day.

All mankind has gone astray, and Isaiah 53:6 tells us that the L-rd has laid on Him the iniquity of us all. As you celebrate this holiday, you must examine your own heart to see if you are in the faith. Are you seeking to live a life of separation that will glorify Messiah, or are you so wrapped up in this world that it is difficult for anyone to tell you are a believer in Messiah?

In closing, I would remind believers that we are to be unleavened bread in this perverse world. Our light is to so shine that all men will see our Father and give Him glory. Remember this: we may be the only unleavened bread that some sinner will see during his lifetime. We do not want to miss the chance to glorify our Father by our testimony.

If you are reading this now and your spirit does not bear witness with our Father's Spirit that you are his child, I implore you to flee from the wrath to come. The Scripture says to repent and believe on Yeshua the Messiah, and you will receive salvation.

Shavuot (Pentecost)

The Feast of Weeks

INTRODUCTION

The Feast of First Fruits (Lev. 23:9-14) sets the stage for the Feast of Weeks. This holiday was called Pentecost (Greek for fifty) by the Greek-speaking Jewish people at the time of Messiah. Since Greek was the language of commerce, many Jewish people spoke it. On the day of the Feast of Firstfruits the counting of the Omer starts. The Omer is the sheaf offering that the priest waves before the L-rd G-d, who is also our Creator and Sustainer at the Feast of Firstfruits. In the tradition of the Temple, the priests, and the Sadducees the counting of the Omer starts on the day of the Feast of Firstfruits, which is the Sunday during the week-long Feast of Unleavened Bread. The Omer is counted for forty-nine days; then, on the fiftieth day the Feast of Shavuot is celebrated.

During this period (starting on the Feast of Firstfruits) there are seven Sabbaths. The first Sabbath occurs seven days after the start of the counting of the Omer (the day that the counting starts is the first day) and the seventh occurs on the forty-ninth day of the counting of the Omer. For example, in the year 2003 (Hebrew calendar 5763), the Feast of Firstfruits occurred on April 20th (Hebrew calendar 18th of Nisan), and the feast of Shavuot occurred on June 8 (Hebrew calendar 8th of Sivan). Seven full weeks of Sabbaths equal seven times seven days. Seven is the number of completion in the Scriptures, and this time period reflects completion time's completion. We will explain the subject of this completion later in this book.

The celebration for the Feast of Weeks starts on the fiftieth day. Fifty days after the Israelites had gained their freedom from the armies of Pharaoh by passing through the Red Sea, they received the law at Mount Sinai. Israel considered this day to be the day of the giving of the law and therefore the legal beginning of her nation. The number fifty is the number of the Jubilee, which signifies freedom. During the Jubilee year, any Israelites who had been in bondage to aliens or temporary residents or who sold themselves as hired workers to fellow Israelites, received their freedom and were returned to their own clan and their own property.

This feast is also known by other names. Exodus 23:16, lists three annual pilgrimage festivals. The name used there is "Yom ha-Katzir," meaning the Day of Harvest. Exodus 34:22, calls it "Chag ha-Shavuous;" the Feast of Weeks; and Numbers 28:26 calls this feast "Yom ha-Bikkurim," the Day of Firstfruits. The New Covenant Scriptures refer to this holiday as Pentecost. They are all the same feast, namely the Feast of Weeks in Leviticus 23:15–22.

Pentecost is considered to be the birth of the Church and the beginning of the visual fulfillment of the covenant of grace promised by our Father and explained by the prophet Jeremiah in 31:31ff. This holiday celebrates the arrival of the Comforter that Messiah had promised. The Comforter is the Holy Spirit, who is the Spirit of the Father and the Son. Under this New Covenant, He would now make His permanent habitation in the hearts of all true believers, who would become His temple.

The Holy Spirit quickens the sinners who are being drawn by our Father to repent of their sin and call on the name of Messiah for salvation. It is the Holy Spirit who is constantly with believers, permanently indwelling them and acting as a restraint and guide in all situations. He corrects our waywardness with the rod and gives us comfort with His staff. Messiah Yeshua tells us that He will never leave us nor forsake us, because, His Holy Spirit, is constantly with us (Hebrews 13:5).

When we are indwelt by the Holy Spirit, we become spiritual creations - old things have passed away; behold all things become new (II Cor. 5:17). In addition to being here on earth, we are also seated in the heavenly realms with Messiah (Eph. 2:6). It is the Holy Spirit who teaches us not to be conformed to this world but to be transformed by the renewing of our mind, so that we may prove what is that good and acceptable and perfect will of G-d (Rom. 12:2).

It is the Holy Spirit who teaches us the two great Commandments on which all the law and the prophets hang. This Spirit teaches us to love the L-rd our G-d with all our heart, with all our soul, and with all our mind. This Spirit also teaches us that we are to love our neighbor as ourselves (Matthew 22:37ff.). To accomplish these things, the Spirit teaches us to be holy, merciful, kind, and loving. It is the Holy Spirit who teaches us that, even though we once practiced sin, we are now to cut sin's clinging tentacles and seek the kingdom of our L-rd and His righteousness.

It is the Holy Spirit who gives various gifts to the spiritually reborn children of our L-rd , so that they not only become more conformed to Messiah, but they also give glory to Him for paying for their sin. It is the Holy Spirit's indwelling believers which gives them sweet peace and communion that passes all understanding of natural man. It is the Holy Spirit who teaches believers to glory in Messiah and not in themselves. It is the Holy Spirit who is taking sinful Jewish people and sinful Gentiles and making one new creature in Messiah Yeshua (Eph. 2 11-22).

It is our Father, Messiah Yeshua our Savior, and their Spirit the Holy Spirit, who provide the complete salvation for all who come to Messiah. They are one comprised of more than one. The Father draws men for salvation: The Son, who pays for their sin, announces to all men "come unto me all you that labor and are heavy laden and I will give you rest". The Holy Spirit convicts men of their sin, and applies salvation to their heart upon their repentance. They are three separate entities, all thinking and working as one. They are referred as an "Echad" one comprised of more than one in Israel's doxology, the Shema (Deut 6:4-6).

These people are called a new creation (II Cor. 5:17). Matthew 5:14 also calls them the light of the world. The light they have is not their own light but is the light of the Holy Spirit in them.

The Holy Spirit has brought people to salvation from the dawn of time. In times before the Spirit was resident permanently in the hearts of believers, He still brought people to salvation because of the future work of Messiah rather than in the already accomplished work of Messiah as He does in this age. Read Hebrews 11, the book of Jonah, I Kings 19:18, and Rom. 11:1-4.

This holiday celebrates the work of the Holy Spirit in ages past, present and future. The day will come in the future when the Holy Spirit will convict Israel as a nation of her sin. She will turn and look upon Messiah and mourn for Him as one morns for an only Son. It is then that she will say "Baruch Haba B'Shem Ado-ai, blessed is He who comes in the name of the L-rd." The physical nation will join the spiritual nation of Israel, and the people will become evangelists to the nations just as they were after Messiah was sacrificed. Think about these things as we proceed.

Shavuot (Pentecost)

THREE QUESTIONS AND THEIR ANSWERS

How was the Feast of Weeks established?

How was and is the Feast of Weeks celebrated?

What are the implications of the Feast of Weeks under the New Covenant?

How was the Feast of Weeks established?

This feast was established by our L-rd in His message to Moses recorded in Leviticus 23. From the day after the Sabbath, the day one brought the sheaf of the wave offering, he would count off seven full weeks. He would count off 50 days up to the day after the seventh Sabbath, and then present an offering of new grain to your Father. From wherever he lives, he would bring two loaves made of 2/10 of an ephah of fine flour, baked with yeast, as a wave offering of first fruits to your Father

With this bread he would present seven male lambs, each a year old and without defect, one bull and two rams. They would be burnt offerings to the L-rd, together with the grain offerings and drink offerings—and offering made by fire, an aroma pleasing to your L-rd. Than he would offer one male goat for a sin offering and two lambs, each a year old, for fellowship offering.

The priest was to wave the two lambs before our L-rd as a wave offering, together with the bread of the first fruits. They were a sacred offering to your L-rd for the priest. On that same day the Israelite was to proclaim a sacred assembly and do no regular work. This was to be a lasting ordinance for the generations to come, wherever one lived (Lev. 23:15-21).

How was and is the Feast of Weeks celebrated?

This was the second time in the year that all males of Israel were required to come to the Temple and appear before the L-rd. Three feasts were celebrated at Passover, and three feasts were celebrated together at Tabernacles; but the Feast of Weeks was a celebration by itself that lasted for only one day. It should be noted that it did not stand alone, but in actuality it was connected to Passover through the Feast of First Fruits.

The Feast of Weeks was connected to the Feast of First Fruits by the counting of the omer of barley that was waved before Israel's L-rd who was also her King. The Feast of Weeks was celebrated on the fiftieth day of that counting. The counting was to start on the day after the Sabbath. The Scriptures are unclear as to which Sabbath was to be used.

The Pharisees and the Falashas (Ethiopian Jews) believe that the Sabbath being referred to is the first day of the feast of unleavened bread. The Sadducees and the Karaites believed that the Sabbath referred to was the regular weekly Sabbath that occurred sometime after the first day of the feast of unleavened bread. Since the Almighty One did not set down a specific date for the Feast Of Weeks, its actual celebration date is unclear.

The Pharisees were and are people who believe that our Father gave Moses an oral law in addition to the law written on the tablets of stone. They believe that the sum total of the laws given to Israel were 613. They believe that these are the laws that were eventually codified in approximately 175 AD. It is known as the Mishna, which is one part of the Talmud. The Pharisees also believe in a resurrection and an eternal kingdom as a reward for the righteous.

For the most part, the Sadducees and the Karaites do not believe in the authority of the rabbis and believe without equivocation that our Father never gave Moses an oral law. The Karaites believe that there will be a resurrection and an eternal kingdom reward for the righteous. The Sadducees do not believe in a resurrection or an eternal kingdom. The party of the Sadducees was led by the Temple priests, scribes, and large landholders, while the Pharisees were generally led by local spiritual leaders in towns and cities.

The Sadducees believed primarily in forgiveness from sin through sacrifice while the Pharisees believed in forgiveness from sin by deeds of righteousness in addition to sacrifice. After the Temple was destroyed, the Pharisees expanded upon their doctrine of earning righteousness. This system is in common vogue in Judaism today.

Most Rabbis are Pharisees; and therefore, their means of determining the date to celebrate this holiday are followed at this time. While this is predominant, there are also groups that follow the reckoning of the Sadducees; in effect, we have two groups in Judaism celebrating this holiday at different times.

During the times of the Temple, the worshippers would come with the best offerings of their first fruits. They brought whatever they were harvesting at that time as a free will offering unto our Father. The Scripture is clear that there was to be one special offering above all others at this time. That offering was to be two loaves of bread that were to be made with yeast and newly harvested wheat flour. The loaves were to be already baked when they were brought to the Temple. The worshipers took very seriously the admonition that the wheat flour was to be finely sifted. Some accounts tell us that the flour was actually sifted twelve or thirteen times before it was used to make the offering. The amount of flour that was used indicates that there were two loaves that were approximately twelve inches by twenty one inches by three inches high. These loaves were made with leaven and they were waved up and down and back and forth before the altar.

During the Feast Of Weeks the book of Ruth is read in the synagogues. This book tells the story of Ruth, a Moabitess, who forsakes the evil of her people and joins herself to the Father and Creator of Israel. Boaz as a kinsman redeemer then redeems her. He is a relative of her mother-in-law Naomi.

We must remember that leaven was never used in any other offerings before our L-rd. Leaven is a symbol of sin. On this festival we are being shown that, the Sovereign L-rd and King of Israel takes the loaves with leaven as an offering, He is also taking sinful people unto Himself. He has always done this from the dawn of time right up to this day.

It was not until after the destruction of the Temple that the rabbis started to speak about this convocation as being the day of the giving of the law at Mount Sinai. While this may be true, it is not enunciated absolutely clearly in Scripture. The giving of the law was a far-reaching spiritual event that established the people as separate unto their L-rd. Jewish writers have compared this to a wedding between the L-rd and His people Israel. Tradition says that Torah was offered to all the nations, but only Israel would accept its restrictions. Tradition also states that King David was born and died on the Feast Of Weeks. There is no Biblical proof to back up either of these assertions.

During this holiday, homes and synagogues are usually decorated with flowers, fruit, and greens. In very religious circles people will stay up all through the night reading from the books of the law. In addition to reading part of the law some will also include the prophets, other writings, and some parts of the Talmud. The Ten Commandments are also read during the service for this holiday. It is very common for children to put on plays with colorful costumes depicting the story of Ruth.

Alfred Edersheim gives us a good description of what actually transpired in the Temple during the Feast of First Fruits. First, two live lambs were waved before the L-rd. After their sacrifice the breast and the shoulder, or the principal parts of each, were laid beside the two loaves and waved forward and backward and up and down. After the loaves were waved, the people brought their own free-will offerings just as our L-rd had prospered them. There was then and is now in religious homes a special festive meal during the afternoon and evening. During this meal Jewish people welcome others to join them as our L-rd's special guests.

What are the implications of the Feast of Weeks under the New Covenant?

Messiah spoke of the fulfillment of the Feast of Weeks during His last Passover supper. John 14:16-17 says "And I will ask the Father, and He will give you another counselor to be with you forever-the spirit of truth. The world cannot accept Him, because it neither sees Him nor knows Him. But you know Him,, for He lives with you and will be in you." John 14:26 says: "But the counselor, the Holy Spirit, whom the Father will send in My name, will teach you all things and will remind you of everything I have said to you."

John 15:26-27 "When the counselor comes, whom I will send to you from the Father, the spirit of truth who goes out from the Father, He will testify about me; but you must also testify, for you have been with me from the beginning."

Messiah said to them, "This is what I told you while I was still with you: everything must be fulfilled that is written about me in the Law of Moses, the prophets and the Psalms. Then he opened their minds so they could understand the Scriptures. He told them, this is what is written: Messiah will suffer and rise from the dead on the third day, and repentance and forgiveness of sins will be preached in His name to all the nations, beginning at Jerusalem. You are witnesses of these things. I am going to send you what my Father has promised; but stay in this city until you have been clothed with power from on high" (Luke 24:44-49).

Fifteen Hundred years after the giving of the law on Mount Sinai, Adonai revisited His people Israel in Jerusalem. He used some of the same miraculous signs that He displayed at Mt. Sinai to gain the attention of the people. Luke records the events in Acts 2:1-21

"When the day of Pentecost came, they were all together in one place. Suddenly a sound like the blowing of a violent wind came from heaven and filled the whole house where they were sitting. They saw what seemed to be tongues of fire that separated and came to rest on each of them. All of them were filled with the Holy Spirit and began to speak in other tongues as the spirit enabled them.

"Now there were staying in Jerusalem Jews from every nation under Heaven who feared G-d. When they heard this sound, a crowd came together in bewilderment, because each one heard them speaking in his own language. Utterly amazed, they asked: are not all these men who are speaking Galileans? Then how is it that each of us hears them in his own native language? Parthians, Medes and Elamites; residence of Mesopotamia, Judea and Cappadocia, Pontus and Asia, Phrygia and Pamphylia, Egypt and the parts of Libya near Cyrene; visitors from Rome (both Jews and converts to Judaism) Cretans and Arabs – we hear them declaring the wonders of G-d in our own tongues! Amazed and perplexed, they asked one another, what does this mean. Some, however, made fun of them and said; they have had too much wine.

"Then Peter stood up with the 11, raised his voice and addressed the crowd: fellow Jews and all of you who are in Jerusalem let me explain this to you; listen carefully to what I say. These men are not drunk, as you suppose. It is only nine in the morning! Know this is what was spoken by the prophet Joel: in the last days, our Father says, I will pour out my spirit on all people. Your sons and your daughters will prophesy, your young man will see visions, even old men will dream dreams. Even on my servants, both men and women, I will pour out my spirit in those days, and they will prophesy. I will show wonders in heaven above & on the earth below, blood and fire and pillows of smoke. The sun will be turned to darkness and the moon to blood before the coming of the great and glorious day of the L-rd. And everyone who calls on the name of the L-rd will be saved."

The Older Covenant that was given to Moses on Mount Sinai was closed on this day. That covenant could never bring people to the point of holiness and acceptability to our Almighty Father. They were all dead in their trespass and sins and never became a kingdom of priests. This holiday is a condemnation of man's so-called free will and exultation of our Father's free grace. Israel as a nation was not able to complete the requirements of the law in and of herself. However, because of His free grace, our Father reserved some of Israel and some Gentiles unto salvation during the time period covered by the Older Covenant.

The Feast of Weeks is part and parcel of and irrevocably tied to Passover. There is a cause and effect relationship: because one thing happened something else had to occur. It is absolutely fantastic. Messiah Yeshua said that after He was sacrificed and returned to His father He would send the Comforter to this earth to help all believers. This is what was accomplished at the Feast of Weeks. Our Father and our Messiah sent their Holy Spirit to be resident on this earth. When the Holy Spirit is permanently resident on this earth He is able to strengthen all true believers so that they will follow after Messiah and have a victorious life.

The ultra orthodox Jewish people say that, if just one Jewish man can complete all the 613 laws of the Sabbath Messiah will return. That is highly unlikely. It has not been done for 2000 years; and some of the laws are specifically for women and others pertain specifically to the Temple. The fact is incontrovertible: Yeshua, (Jesus) is the Messiah, and He fulfilled the Older Covenant and had the only Authority to establish the New Covenant. Neither the ecclesiastical authority (the Sanhedrin) nor the civil authority (the Roman government) could find any legal fault in Him. He was the perfect sacrifice for sin and was approved by His Father. The Scripture tells us, therefore, there is no condemnation in any who are in Messiah Jesus (Romans 8:1).

The rabbis tell us that this holiday, the Feast of Weeks, is an Atzeret, a solemn assembly that is tied to Passover. In other words one is incomplete without the other. They are tied together through the Feast of Unleavened Bread and the counting of the omer. In truth the rabbis do not know how right they really are. Messiah was sacrificed to pay for the sins of all the people. That was not something that was done in isolation. It had to lead to something, and that something was the new creation.

The new creation is a spiritual creation that was the fulfillment of the New Covenant promised in Jeremiah 31:31. In this covenant the Almighty One says He will do all the work, and the sinner to whom He chooses to reveal Himself to will be the recipient. The recipient does nothing except what the Revealer has revealed. Once the Revealer opens the sinner's eyes and unplugs his ears, he sees his sinfulness and calls upon the name of Messiah to be forgiven.

Once Messiah became the perfect sacrifice, something had to be done with the people for whom His sacrifice was going to be efficacious for. Therefore, the New Covenant was activated on the same day that the Older Covenant had been given. The new replaced the old in its entirety. "Old things have passed away behold all things have become new" (II Cor. 5:17). The newness was not that under the New Covenant man is saved by grace, because the only way man was ever saved is by our Father's grace alone. Rather, the newness occurs because once man receives salvation, he is indwelt by the Holy Spirit on this earth; and he is immediately seated in the heavenlies (Ephesians 2:6).

The New Covenant Scriptures tell us that there is no difference between Jew and Gentile; our Father is over all. Because of our Father's own free sovereign will He chooses to reveal Himself to certain people. The Scriptures tell us that all have sinned and come short of the glory of G-d (Rom 3:23). All men are sinners and on their way to the lake of the everlasting burnings. It is because of our Father's great mercy that He chooses to save some from that fate.

The New Covenant Scriptures starting the new creation, had to be made with someone; and it also had to have a purpose. The two loaves of bread made with yeast are very important. The loaves were baked with newly harvested wheat that was sifted many times. Notice that one was baked with wheat and the other baked with barley. Both loaves were equal in their ingredients. Yeast was an indicator of sin, and both loaves were baked with yeast.

These loaves were also waved together before the L-rd. This indicates that the recipients of the salvation that was provided by Messiah Jesus through His sacrifice would be comprised of two separate classes of people, namely Jews and Gentiles. The fact that these loaves are waved up and down and back and forth indicate to me that these two classes of people will be drawn from the whole earth. The Older Covenant symbol has become a glorious reality under the New Covenant. A new entity, the Church, comprised of sinful Jews and sinful Gentiles, receives salvation by the shed blood of her common Bridegroom.

Even though it is true that we will be presented to Messiah without having spot or wrinkle, while we are on this earth we are sinners. Perfection will never be attained either by the Church as a whole or by individuals separately. Perfection is found only in Messiah Himself.

Isa. 61:1 says: "The Spirit of the L-rd is upon me; because He has anointed Me to preach good tidings to the meek; He has sent me to bind up the brokenhearted, to proclaim liberty to the captives, and the opening of the prison to them who are bound." This is exactly what every believer should be doing in one form or another. We do this because we are the body and bride of Messiah. The three thousand Jewish men that were baptized at the Feast of Weeks recorded in Acts 2 returned to their own communities and spread the gospel to both Jews and Gentiles alike. Today it is our responsibility to share the gospel of our Father's free grace to all we meet.

In the Temple there was a wall called Chel. Gentiles were not permitted to go past that wall in their worship. That wall has been broken down; the two loaves are now one. Out of the Jews separately and the Gentiles separately, our Father has made one new man in Messiah (Ephesians 2:15). The implication under the New Covenant for this holiday is one of brotherhood. Each part of the new body is to have respect for the other and operate for the glory of the One who granted salvation to both of them. This holiday should be celebrated in its fullness showing that the old has gone away and has been replaced by the new. The New Covenant salvation is open to anyone who will come, repent of his sins and believe on Yeshua the Messiah. Scripture tells us that he will receive salvation.

CONCLUSION

The apostles were waiting in Jerusalem for the Comforter to come, as Messiah had promised. Pentecost memorializes the giving of the Holy Spirit with the law of the L-rd being written on the heart of every believer. Under the Older Covenant the pilgrims that came to the Temple could bring only fruits of crops that were grown in the land, as an offering unto our L-rd. Under the New Covenant it is our Almighty Father Himself who provides the first fruits of salvation. That first fruit was Yeshua- Jesus the Messiah.

During the Feast of Weeks the worshippers read about the glory of the Lord in Ezekiel 1. Ezekiel says in 36:27;"I will put my spirit within you and cause you to walk in my statutes and you shall keep my ordinances and do them." The feast of Pentecost is celebrated as the birthday of the Church, because our Father's law was placed in the hearts of all believers on that day by the Holy Spirit. Since Messiah rose to be with His Father, His Spirit and His Father's Spirit remain permanently with all believers. When a person becomes one with Messiah he is filled with Messiah's Spirit, and the spirit of Yeshua will remain with him until he leaves this earth.

The identifying mark of a true believer is not someone who knows about our Father's will but someone who does His will because the Father's Spirit is within him. A believer under the new covenant is able to live out our Father's word because our Father has given that believer the power to do so. Once a true believer receives the Spirit of our Father our King he will press toward the mark for the high calling that is in Messiah. The Older Covenant scriptures told people how they were to live, but they did not give them the power to live according to our Father's law. Under the New Covenant all believers are a kingdom of priests because we are in Messiah who is our High Priest. As priests we are required to do daily sacrifices to mortify the flesh that would so easily draw us away from our Savior and Messiah.

Messiah has already told us that He will never leave us nor forsake us (Heb. 13:5). Israel spoke rashly when in exodus 19:8 she said that all that G-d had spoken she would do. We who are indwelt by the Holy Spirit have been told that we can do all things through Messiah who strengthens us. Our covenant is based on better promises. We are partakers of an unconditional covenant. Our salvation is not based on our ability to keep that unconditional covenant. Rather, our salvation is assured because we are the bride of the One who has already completed that covenant to its fullest extent.

In celebrating this holiday correctly, all believers have a chance to make Israel envious. Israel looks forward to this holiday being completed. The believer can say truly to natural Israel that this holiday has been completely fulfilled in the Messiah of Israel, Yeshua the righteous one. We can say to them, "Come unto the author and finisher of our faith who is bone of your bone and flesh of your flesh."

The Feast of Trumpets

INTRODUCTION

When the L-rd our G-d established the Feast of Trumpets, He did so in a very succinct manner: "On the first day of the seventh month you are to have a day of rest, a sacred assembly commemorated with trumpet blasts. Do no regular work, but present an offering made to our Father by fire" (Lev.23:24). Neither in the record of the first occurrence of this feast in the Scripture nor in any subsequent Scripture record, does our Father make it clear why the trumpets were blown. I would suggest to you that the trumpets were blown to alert all who read and knew the Holy Scriptures that there would be a time in the future that would astound the thinking of any rational human being. There would be a time when the Messiah of Israel would come to this earth to fulfill all Scripture that had been written about Him. He would come to bear the sins of all people.

Year after year the Levites blew the trumpets in the temple and the synagogues for this convocation, and no one could say with any scriptural authority why they were being blown. According to Jewish tradition there are four days that are celebrated as new year days. Each of them had its own function in the economy of Israel. Each is explained in the Talmud in Rosh Hashanah 1:1 and following.

The first of Nisan is the new year for the religious calendar; Passover therefore, is the first festival celebrated for the new year. This religious calendar is also the calendar for listing the reign of kings. For example, if a king ascended to the throne one week before the first of Nisan, the first of Nisan would be in the second year of his reign.

The second day celebrated as a new year day is the first of Elul. On this day the individuals in Israel gave tithes for all the cattle born during the previous year.

The third New Year starts on the first of Tishri. It is the new year for the civil calendar, Sabbatical and Jubilee years, and for the tithing of fruit and vegetables. The trumpets for the Jubilee and/or Sabbatical year are not blown on this day to free people from their bondage; the trumpet blast in a Sabbatical or Jubilee year indicates that from this day forward, for the next ten days, plowing and planting were forbidden. It was the religious new year, the day in which all the world was judged. It is called the day of the trumpet blast, The Feast of Trumpets. Rosh Hashanah, meaning "the beginning of the year" is the name of this convocation.

The fourth New Year starts on either the first day or the fifteenth day of Shevat, depending on whether one follows the school of Hillel or the school of Shammai. It is the new year for tithing all of the bounty of the trees.

The only new year that is celebrated with any regularity today in Judaism is the one that starts on the first of Tishri, it is called Rosh Hashanah or the Feast of Trumpets.

Israel looked forward to both the Sabbatical and Jubilee years. In addition to their historical significance, they were a foreshadowing of what was to come. In the future there would be a time when the L-rd our G-d would grant permanent spiritual freedom instead of temporary temporal freedom. It would be called the acceptable year of our L-rd.

Isaiah 61:1-3 says, "The Spirit of the sovereign L-rd is upon me, because He hath anointed me to preach good tidings unto the meek; He hath sent me to bind up the brokenhearted, to proclaim liberty to the captives, and the opening of the prison to them that are bound; to proclaim the acceptable year of our L-rd, and the day of His vengeance; to comfort all that mourn; to appoint unto those who mourn in Zion, to give unto them beauty for ashes, the oil of joy for mourning, the garment of praise for the spirit of heaviness, that they might be called trees of righteousness, the planting of the L-rd that He might be glorified" .

Cotton Mather, a Puritan preacher from New England, longed for the salvation of the Jewish people. The Theology of Mission in the Puritan Tradition, states (p.247): "This day from the dust, where I lay prostrate before the L-rd my G-d, I lifted up my cries . . . for the conversion of the Jewish nation, and for my own having the Happiness, at sometime or other, to Baptize a Jew that should by my ministry be brought home unto His L-rd."

Mather longed to proclaim to the Jews of his day that Messiah has brought the permanent spiritual freedom about which Isaiah wrote. I, too, long to proclaim the same good news. I like to imagine that if one is very quiet, he can hear a heavenly trumpet blast announcing that there is to be a Jubilee for a lost soul who is brought "home unto his L-rd." Let me share with you the testimony of one such lost sheep of Israel.

Rachmiel Frydland was a lovely man and he and I became friends in 1973. He was a survivor of the terrors of the Holocaust and tells his own story in this way. September 1, 1939 was a beautiful day in Warsaw Poland. I was walking along Nowolipki Street heading toward the Jewish business district, when the big rooftop sirens began to wail. I thought it was another air raid test and then before I walked ½ block further on, I heard the drone of airplane engines and then the heart stopping roar of exploding bombs. Warsaw was under attack by German bombers. World War II had begun.

I quickly took shelter in a nearby house and then wondered what I could possibly do. Where could a Jewish Polish citizen find safety from the advancing German military machine with its slave labor, starvation, torture and murder for the so-called" inferior races".

The poor Jewish community where I was born and lived was small and not able to maintain a cheder (Jewish day school). My father was very devout felt that it was his duty himself to instruct his five children, my four sisters and his only son, in the faith of his fathers. He hired an instructor for us but then was not able to financially keep it up. I was sent to the yeshiva in Chelm and then went to study in Warsaw, the capital.

As I studied, perturbing questions began to creep into my thinking at first they were little but later they became ever larger. Were the Gentiles as terrible as my teachers said? Why did Christians follow the teachings of our Jewish prophets? Why must the school discipline be so strict and unfeeling?

I encountered some financial difficulties and began to sell clothing items like a peddler on the street to earn money. This disqualifies me from ever becoming a rabbi. At 17 I was on my own in Warsaw and was taken in by a Jewish tailor and his family. My new friends encouraged me to go with them to a meeting hall where Gentile Christians were seeking to convert Jews. They said I could help them answer the missionaries claim that Jesus was really the Messiah of the Jewish people. I agreed to go

After the meeting I talked with the preacher about the prophecies for the long-awaited Messiah of Israel. I was able to answer all his questions except one. Daniel 9:24-26 told us of Messiah's departure from Jerusalem. All the Jewish commentaries I studied were not able to help me give him an answer. The passage which perplexed me reads as follows: 70 weeks are determined by thy people and upon thy holy city, to finish the transgression, and to make an end of sins, and to make reconciliation for iniquity, and to bring in everlasting righteousness, and to seal up the vision and the prophecy, and to anoint the most holy. Know therefore and understand that from the going forth of the commandment to restore and rebuild Jerusalem unto the Messiah the Prince shall be seven weeks, and threescore and two weeks: the street shall be built again in the wall, even in troubled times. And after threescore and two weeks shall Messiah be cut off but not for Himself.

Anything I knew about this passage was all gathered from what other people had taught me and their logic and answers soon melted away. The prophetic passages which appeared to be fulfilled in Jesus were too numerous to be explained away. As I admitted this to myself I was determined to read the New Testament to find out about this Jesus.

I obtained a copy of the New Testament in Hebrew and carefully compared the references I found in the Tenach and slowly and clearly it began to run to dawn on me that the New Testament was a continuation of the Old Testament. One evening in 1937 I sat in a meeting composed wholly of Jewish people who profess Jesus as the Messiah. The speaker was a Gentile woman who spoke compellingly and with great understanding about the Temple of Jerusalem she traced its great significance for the faith of Israel, showing that its appointments and structure or divine object lessons, pointing to man's sinful condition and God's provision for forgiveness, culminating in the sacrifice of the Messiah for the forgiveness of sins. So, that is why Messiah had to be cut off as Daniel had foretold! "How is it," I asked myself, "that a Gentile woman knows more about the Bible and its significance than I, a student of the Yeshiva? At this very meeting I prayed and asked Messiah Jesus to become my atonement and Savior.

I had been a believer for two years when the war broke out. Warsaw shook under more and more bombs. Food became scarce and the electricity and water supply failed. Along with several other young Jewish believers in Messiah, I went to help defend the city. Because I did not want to use a gun, I was given physical work. Within a month the city was crushed in the triumphant Germans marched in.

I decided to leave the city and seek farm work with friends to the north. With a certificate in hand given to me by my pastor I set out to cross a burning city. Reaching the outskirts, I was stopped by a soldier. "Are you a Jew! He grabbed a shovel slammed it into my back, and knocked me into a ditch. I was ordered with my fellow Jews to dig graves for dead horses. It was my first taste of Nazi brutality, but actually mild in comparison what awaited so many others.

That night I escaped in the darkness to join my friends. They received me gladly and fed me but in the short time new restrictive laws against Jews forced me to leave. I returned to Warsaw and discovered one of my sisters had died of typhus and the wall had been built around the Jewish section. It decided to walk the 150 miles southeast to my native village because Jews were not allowed to travel in public: vehicles anymore.

My parents could hardly believe I was still alive when I arrived at my family home in mid-December. One of my sisters also returned home, and we settled down, hoping to wait out the war. We knew, however that our blue-and-white armbands marking us as Jews, were a constant hazard to our lives. I was forced to work with slave laborers, building a road, and managed to escape when starvation swept in. Home again, my mother told me that I must stop telling my Jewish friends about the Messiah. But the spreading pall of suffering and death caused people to reach out for some hope for answer for the dreaded future.

One day my sister came to me." I read your Bible," she said, "and I heard your discussions. I believe, and if God gives us peaceful days, I want to be baptized. "My mother came to me and said, "I have watched you and you are a different person. I was reading your New Testament and I don't see anything wrong with this Jesus. Why are our rabbis so much against him? My father never admitted anything to me. However, he stopped hiding my Bible and rebuking me for speaking about Jesus. He began secretly to read the Bible.

The blossoming faith of my family was a great blessing to me as death drew nearer in 1942. I saw trucks and trains loaded with Jewish people rolling toward the extermination camp at Sobibor. One by one and village by village they disappeared. My father, my mother, my sisters, my newly wedded wife, and all other relatives except my brother-in-law perished. At the end of August the order came for me to go. I was given permission by the Mayor of our village to say goodbye to my parents, who at that time had not yet been called. I fled to the woods, and though time and again I was captured, by miracle after miracle God enabled me to survive.

Once, alone in the woods in the biting cold of winter, exhausted and discouraged, my whole being seemed to cry out: "Why are we so persecuted ?" I was convinced that the companions who had been with me just a few days before had been caught, and lived no more. I, too, was ready to die. But there still remained the Lord, the same yesterday and today. He began to speak to me. "You have enough of my grace. Had not Job enough? Had not Paul enough?" The still small voice of God spoke softly to me. Overcome with tears, I yielded and decided to live as long as the Lord will allow me to live, and to work for Him. Confident that God was with me I rose up and left those woods.

As I moved from place to place, Gentile Christians often risked their lives by hiding and feeding me. One of my bitterest experiences, however, was the discovery that many German Christians, though they knew of the Nazi atrocities against the Jews, would not help. "It is our government, and we must obey," they said.

In late 1944, by hiding in cemeteries, deserted churches, and the homes of fearful friends, I was one of the few surviving Jews in Warsaw outside the ghetto. In that enclosure there were 5000 Jews the last of Warsaw's original 500,000. By God's enabling I secretly slipped into the ghetto and was able to speak comfort to a few of the Jewish believers still alive. Other Jewish brethren heard the message and believed in Messiah Jesus. My friends in the ghetto insisted that I leave. They said that if God had preserved me thus far, I would be a witness to the woes they now experience. At the end of the war, I could tell the story of their suffering. I was probably one of the last to leave the ghetto. It was only shortly afterwards that the Germans obliterated the entire Jewish area.

Time seemed to drag slowly. There were nights when a Christian family would risk their lives by sheltering a Jew. Once, in the shop of the Christian undertaker, I slept in a coffin. There are other times when a barn provided my shelter. In all that time there was the assurance that God wanted me to live. As long as He wanted it, I was ready. And finally the day came when I was no longer hunted and condemned for being a Jew. In January 1945 Russian troops entered Warsaw the automatic death sentence for Jews was lifted.

After the war I left Poland and went to England to study. With my training behind me, I came to the United States to share in a witness for Messiah among my own people. Then, for four years, I lived in Israel serving as a pastor to Israeli believers in Messiah and sharing my witness with my brethren there. In Israel I met my wife, she was also a Jewish believer in the Messiah. She had suffered through the Nazi occupation of France and had survived to immigrate to Israel

Words fail to describe what my heart feels. Ordered by the power and greatness of the God of Daniel, King Darius wrote a decree to his dominions which perhaps describes best the order and reverence that I feel for what God has done for me.

… For He is The living God enduring forever; His kingdom shall never be destroyed, and his dominion shall be to the end. He delivers and He rescues, He works signs and wonders in heaven and on the earth, He who has saved Daniel from the power of the lions. (Daniel 6:26-27)

From my harrowing experience, I see that men who reject Messiah are capable of bringing hell on earth. But surely God has not abandoned mankind. He has a plan for every person who will trust Him . The Bible, which has guided and sustained me thus far, promises that peace and justice will fill the earth only when the Prince of Peace returns. He is the only hope of mankind, and I know that He will come, because He has proved His great love and His miraculous power to me. Will you not also trust Him, my friend?

THREE QUESTIONS AND THEIR ANSWERS

As we deal with the ramifications of this festival for believers today, we will ask and answer three questions, and then offer a conclusion.

How was the Feast of Trumpets established?

The Feast of Trumpets

This convocation was instituted by the L-rd our G-d in Leviticus 23:23 ff. and Numbers 29:1-6: "the L-rd our G-d said to Moses, 'Say to the Israelites: "On the first day of the seventh month you are to have a day of rest, a sacred assembly commemorated with trumpet blasts".

How was and is the Feast of Trumpets celebrated?

The seventh month was called Tishri and was considered a sabbatical month. This meant that the first day of the month was a Sabbath. It is the only month in which the first day falls on a new moon. It was originally a one-day holiday, but it is now celebrated for two days because in ancient times there was difficulty in discerning when the new moon actually appeared.

There are special instructions for this holiday in Nehemiah 8:1-10. When Nehemiah read and explained the Law, the people wept; but Nehemiah told them not to weep because this was a special day. They were to "go [their] way, eat the fat, and drink the sweet, and send portions unto them for whom nothing is prepared; for this day is holy unto our L-rd. Neither be ye sorry; for the joy of the L-rd is your strength" (Neh.8:10.

Referring to this day, David says in Psalm 81:3-5: "Blow the trumpet at the new moon, at the full moon, on our feast day. For it is a statute for Israel, an ordinance of the Father of Jacob". According to Scripture this holiday was to be a joyous convocation, and the joy of our Father would give the people strength.

As we mentioned earlier, the Scripture tells us that the trumpets (shofar) were to be blown; but it does not tell us why. It is supposed to be a remembrance, but we are not told exactly what is to be remembered. Was Israel supposed to remember things that their Father had done for her in the past? In this day of rest on this convocation was she supposed to reflect on God's goodness? The Scriptures do not tell us.

It seems reasonable that the blowing of the shofar was to remind the people of what their Father had done for them in the past as well as what He would do for them in the future. That would be applicable to each new generation as it looked back on the faithfulness of their Father in its times of trial and tribulation and to the future, wondering what He had in store for it. That is exactly what happened with the Passover. Passover occurred only once, but it was to be celebrated yearly as a remembrance of what our Father our King had done for His people. In celebrating what their Father had done when Israel was in deep trouble, the people would have promise and inspiration that He would do the same thing for them in the future when they were in terrible straits.

There would be a time when all the feasts of Israel would be fulfilled. We are now living in that time period. When the trumpets were blown in the religious calendar year that Messiah was sacrificed, they were blown not only to announce that a new thing had occurred, but they were also blown to show that there was no further need for the sacrifice on the Day of Atonement. The L-rd our G-d had already accepted the sacrifice of Yeshua the Messiah for all the redeemed. In that religious calendar year of Levitical feasts, Messiah would be crucified, suffer for the sins of the redeemed on Calvary's cross, die, spend time in the lower parts of the earth, rise to go to the Father, return to earth, and then go back to be with His Father in Heaven.

During this same period, His body and bride, (the Church) would be formed of both Jewish and Gentile believers. As these people were joined to Messiah, their Father would raise them up to be with Messiah, seated with Him in heavenly places (Eph.2: 6). Jewish believers who were in Jerusalem to celebrate the Feast of Weeks would start to spread the good news of salvation and a new life in Messiah to people as they returned home.

During the Day of Atonement after Messiah was sacrificed, our Father our King gave proof that His glory no longer resided in the Temple. That proof will be explained in the message dealing with Yom Kippur. Rabbinic authority agreed that our Father's Shekinah glory no longer resided in the Temple. That meant that all sacrifices for sin, both corporate and individual, that were brought to the Temple were no longer efficacious.

Because the Temple sacrifices were no longer effective, the rabbis had to make up another system where people might obtain forgiveness for their sin. They devised a system of prayer, charity, good works and study which they said would accomplish the same salvation.

They expanded on Exodus 32:31-33 and Psalm 69:28 to accomplish that end. Exodus 32:31-33 says, "Oh, what a great sin these people have committed! They have made themselves gods of gold. But now, please forgive their sin - but if not, then blot me out of the book you have written.' Our Father replied to Moses, 'Whoever has sinned against me I will blot out of my book.'" (Emphasis added).

Psalm 69:28 says, "May they be blotted out of the book of life and not be listed with the righteous" (emphasis added).

The rabbis changed the meaning of Rosh Hashanah from one of joy (Neh. 8:1-10) in what our Father our King had accomplished for His people to one of a judgment day in which people looked forward to their good works as a means of payment for their sin. They expanded the idea of our Father's book of life to His three books that would tell where each person was in relation to salvation.

According to Jewish tradition the books of judgment were to be opened on this day. How people had acted and how they would act during the ten days between Rosh Hashanah and Yom Kippur (the Day of Atonement) would decide a person's fate for the coming year, as well as for eternity.

The three books that were opened were for three separate groups of people. The first book was for the righteous; the second book was for the unrighteous; and the third book was for those who were neither righteous nor unrighteous. Tradition says that it is possible to move from one book to another. The typical greeting from one person to another during this period is, "May you be inscribed in the book of life for a good year."

The rabbis have their own ideas as to what the blowing of the shofar was to accomplish. Different rabbis give different theories. One of them said that the blowing of the shofar, among other things, was to stir our Father's emotion, so He would move from His judgment seat to His mercy seat. The following prayer was said: "Do thou heed from Heaven's height the shofar blast, and leave thy throne of stern justice for thy seat of mercy."

Rabbinic tradition also states that the sacrifice of Isaac took place on what we now call Rosh Hashanah. Therefore, many people ask the L-rd our G-d to "remember our father Isaac who was bound on the altar; and for his sake grant his offspring mercy. You provided a ram in a thicket, and Isaac was released from the altar." It is their hope that The L-rd will provide His own sacrifice again so that the people can move to the book of the righteous.

Other rabbis say that the blowing of the trumpet also reminds the Jewish people to have faith in the coming of the Messiah. Isaiah 27:13 tells us "and in that day a great trumpet will sound. Those who were perishing in Assyria and those who were exiled in Egypt will come and worship The L-rd on the holy mountain in Jerusalem."

The revered Hebrew teacher Maimonides stated, "The blowing of the Shofar should awake Israel from its slumber, so that they would reflect on their deeds. Remember your Creator. Do not seek vain things. Look to your souls. Each one of you forsake your evil ways and thoughts."

During these ten days, enemies make up, charity is given to the poor, and worshippers make confession and repentance in synagogue prayers. Instead of the shofar's being blown for joy and to give the L-rd glory, it is blown loudly and with alarm.

Some ancient rabbis said the blowing of the ram's horn was for three reasons: one, to call Israel to repentance - to awaken her from her sins; two, to remind our Heavenly Father of His covenant with Israel - to deal gently with her; not according to her deeds but according to His promise to Abraham and three, to confuse Satan, who accuses Israel before our Father on this day and every day.

The Book of Jewish Concepts (page 592) gives nine further reasons why the shofar is blown.

The shofar proclaims the sovereignty of the creator on Rosh Hashanah, the anniversary of Creation.

The shofar warns and stirs the people to amend their life during the ten days of repentance, the time between Rosh Hashanah and Yom Kippur.

The shofar reminds us of the revelation at Mount Sinai when the people said, "We will do and obey."

The shofar brings to mind the prophetic warnings and exhortations.

The shofar was reminiscent of the battle alarm in Judah.

The shofar brings to mind the attempted sacrifice of Isaac.

The shofar inspires the heart with awe and reverence.

The shofar reminds us of the Day of Judgment.

The shofar inspires us with hope for the final restoration of the people of Israel.

These theories have nothing to do with the Scriptural injunction for this convocation. These are man-made reasons with great sounding words that mean nothing in God's plan of salvation.

There are two other traditions connected with Rosh Hashanah that the Jewish people have followed to gain favor with the L-rd G-d. The first one was done during the Middle Ages. Leaders of Jewish communities fasted on the evening of Rosh Hashanah. They believed that, by doing this, they would wipe away one third of Israel's sin. Between Rosh Hashanah and Yom Kippur other people in the community also fasted. They believed that by doing this, another third of Israel's sin would be wiped away. They believed that the last one third of Israel's sin was wiped away with the fast on Yom Kippur. The rabbis do not believe in substitutionary atonement, but they do believe that there is a righteous remnant in Israel that will stave off harsh judgment by our Father against Israel. They also believe that Israel now suffers for the sins of the Gentiles, in addition to her own sins.

The second tradition exists in modern times. Instead of following the Spirit of our Father, orthodox congregations celebrate Tashlich. On the first day of Rosh Hashanah, in the afternoon, members of the congregation gather at bodies of moving water. They turn their pockets inside out, dropping crumbs in the water, as if they are throwing their sins into the depths of the sea. This is based on Micah 7:19 which says that there will be a time in the future when the L-rd our G-d will throw their sins into the depth of the sea. Israel is truly seeking the L-rd our G-d, but not according to knowledge.

The following is part of a litany that Jewish people recite in Hebrew in the synagogue on Rosh Hashanah:

Our Father, our King, we have sinned before thee.

Our Father, our King, we have no king beside thee.

Our Father, our King, renew unto us a happy year.

Our Father, our King, annul every severe decree concerning us.

Our Father, our King, annul the designs of those who hate us.

Our Father, our King, frustrate the counsel of our enemies.

Our Father, our King, stay the mouths of our adversaries and of those who accuse us.

Our Father, our King, remove pestilence, sword, famine, captivity, and destruction from the children of thy covenant.

Our Father, our King, hold back the plague from thine heritage.

Our Father, our King, forgive and pardon all our iniquities.

Our Father, our King, blot out, and cause our transgressions and sins to pass away before thine eyes.

Our Father, our King, efface in thine abundant mercy all records of our guilt.

Our Father, our King, cause us to return unto thee in perfect repentance.

Our Father, our King, send perfect healing to the sick of thy people.

Our Father, our King, repeal the evil sentence of our judgment.

Our Father, our King, remember us in the book of happy life.

Our Father, our King, inscribe us in the book of redemption and salvation.

Our Father, our King, inscribe us in the book of sustenance and maintenance.

Our Father, our King, inscribe us in the book of merit.

Our Father, our King, inscribe us in the book of forgiveness and pardon.

Our Father, our King, cause salvation to spring forth for us.

Our Father, our King, exalt the horn Israel thy people.

Our Father, our King, exalt the horn of thy Messiah.

These words are wonderful words if they express the true desire of the heart. In reality, they mean nothing, if they are only rote repetition of words that man has made up. Words cannot pay for sin - only the sacrifice that the L-rd our G-d requires and provides is sufficient.

Many religious Jewish people quote Ezekiel 33:12; "The righteousness of the righteous man will not save him when he disobeys, and the wickedness of the wicked man will not cause him to fall when he turns from it...." This verse sounds great, but in fact it must be considered in its context, the general requirements for salvation under the Mosaic Covenant.

An acceptable sacrifice is not efficacious if the heart is not broken and contrite, just as a broken and contrite heart is not efficacious if it is not accompanied by a sacrifice that is acceptable to our Father. Under the Older Covenant as well as the New Covenant both elements are required for sin to be forgiven.

The rabbis have added the element of repentance to what was a joyous feast day. They have changed the entire meaning of the atonement. An individual's atonement for his sin was to be a daily affair in his heart and an animal sacrifice whenever he came to the Temple. The Day of Atonement was only for corporate sins of the commonwealth. Now the rabbis make the Feast of Trumpets to be a time for personal repentance, which is not Scriptural.

What are the implications of the Feast of Trumpets under the New Covenant?

All of Israel's feasts and convocations pointed to the sacrifice of Messiah. Numbers 29:2 tells us that the sacrifices were a pleasing aroma to the L-rd. It is significant to note that the sacrifice of Messiah was well pleasing in His Father's sight, for He always did the will of His Father (John 14:10 and 6:38).

Actually, the Son was never more pleasing to the Father than when He cried out, "My Father! My Father! Why hast thou forsaken me?" Voluntarily giving Himself up to death on the cross was the height of our Messiah's submissive obedience to His Father. That is what Philippians means when it says that He became obedient unto death, even the death of the cross.

All believers are now temples of the Holy Spirit, (I Corinthians 3:16). We are to be a sweet savor to our Father, just as Messiah was a sweet savor to His Father. The meat offering at the Temple was the work of the hands of those who made the offering. It was never offered without the drink offering that was a ratification of the sacrifice and a consecration to their spiritual duty. James 2: 18 tells us that our works (the works of our hands) must have faith (spiritual consecration) accompanying them.

When believers celebrate this holiday with joy, they are pointing out to both Israel and the people of the nations that they have the only true Father and King, and the only true salvation. Their message is: "Seek the L-rd our G-d while He may be found and call on Him while He is near." (emphasis added). The shofar declares to those who do not believe in Yeshua the Messiah that the L-rd our G-d will do for them what they cannot do for themselves. Their works are not enough for salvation. All their righteousness is as filthy rags (Isa. 64:5). Believers, by the joy of their declaration in Messiah, say to the rest of the world, "Your heart is deceitful above all things and desperately wicked, who can know it?" (Jer. 17:9). When Israel or the unconverted people in this world say that they can do works of righteousness to tip the scales of judgment in their favor, they are sadly mistaken. Psalm 14:1-3 says that all men are corrupt and their works are abominable; they are altogether filthy; and there is none that does good, no not one. Everyone in the world needs a kinsman redeemer. The good news that believers proclaim, is that this Redeemer has come, and our Father is well pleased with Him and His sacrifice.

What principles about Rosh Hashanah should we apply to ourselves, since we are redeemed? The L-rd our G-d called Isaiah to "cry aloud, spare not, lift up thy voice like a trumpet, and show my people their transgression and the house of Jacob their sins" (Isa. 58:1). We who know and believe the good news of our Father's salvation in Yeshua the Messiah have the same task as the prophets of old. We are to lift our voices as if they were the shofar and call out that the day of rejoicing has come upon the whole earth. In Messiah, our Heavenly Father has made good on all His promises (2 Cor.1:20). Along with Isaiah, we are to "bring good tidings to Zion, go up on a high mountain. You, who bring good tidings to Jerusalem lift up your voice with a shout, lift it up, do not be afraid; say to the towns of Judah, here is your G-d!" (Isa.40:9). The work that pleases our Father is not our own effort to be righteous, but it is belief in the one He has sent (John 6:29). The Apostle Paul tells us in Romans 1:16 "I am not ashamed of the gospel [of Messiah], because it is the power of G-d for the salvation of everyone who believes: first for the Jew, then for the Gentile". We who live in the light of the New Covenant have the awesome privilege and responsibility to blow the ram's horn, to share this good news of what our Father has done with both Jews and Gentiles.

Because salvation is complete, we are to have joy, blow the shofar, and cry out. The sacrifice was once and forever. The work of atonement is done. It never has to and never will be repeated again. In one sense, Messiah partially fulfilled this holiday, so in reality we are to have our joy in Him. In another sense, it will be totally fulfilled when our salvation is fully complete. That will occur when we experientially reside with Him in heaven. We do not have joy specifically for the holiday, but we have joy in the fact that we are a new creation. Rabbinic Judaism must have this day as a somber day, leading to the Day of Atonement. It realizes that a sacrifice must be offered, but it is unable to bring one. In reality, it has only what it can make up; and what it makes up; is not Scriptural.

In contrast to rabbinic Judaism, believers under the New Covenant have an acceptable sacrifice. Our great High Priest was Himself the sacrifice that paid for all of our sins. The sound of the shofar reminds us that our Father our King always has been sovereign, is sovereign now, and always will be sovereign. We who are reborn of the Spirit are perpetually in our Jubilee Year. We are not under the law's commands, but under the law and command of Yeshua.

The blast warns us of the sinfulness of sin and reminds us of the righteousness of Messiah. With the blast of the shofar, the walls of Jericho fell (Josh. 6:20). With its blast the walls of our pride must fall; and we must cast ourselves at Messiah's feet for His protection and our eternal life.

Psalm 89:15, 16 tells us, "Blessed are the people who know the joyful sound; they shall walk, O Father, in the light of thy countenance. In thy name they rejoice all the day, and in thy righteousness shall they be exalted"

CONCLUSION

It does not matter whether you are a believer or an unbeliever; it is a great time to start your life anew. If you read these words and do not know Yeshua as your Messiah and Savior, now is the time to come to Him with a broken and contrite heart, casting all your cares upon Him, for He cares for you. If you are a believer, now is the time for you to covenant with our Father to be a better witness of His freely-given salvation.

Israel as a nation has stumbled at the stumbling stone. In her prayers for this holiday, she wants our L-rd to provide a sacrifice for her just as He provided a sacrifice in place of Isaac. The irony of the whole situation is amazing. Isaiah 60:10 tells us that as a nation her ears are heavy, and her eyes are shut. She can neither see nor hear. In spite of this, there is a remnant of Israel, who has come and continues to come to the knowledge of Yeshua as Messiah. This will continue until the end of this age when all Israel shall be saved.

Another testimony is given by Jewish believers in New York City: Frances was born in New York City and was reared in a religious family. She attended services regularly and lit candles on Friday night. She loved the L-rd her G-d with all her heart, but she confesses that she never truly had peace. Her husband died in 1948, leaving her with two daughters to rear, aged twelve and fifteen. She wondered time and again if her name was written in the book of life. She had no assurance as to where she would spend eternity. This was very bothersome to her, and she delved into many different cults looking for the answer. She tried Jewish science, Christian science, and religious science where she studied metaphysical thought. Even though she studied these religions for over twenty-two years, she never obtained peace in her heart. Her life was empty, purposeless, and lonely.

When her mother was dying of back cancer, Frances had contact with born-again believers in Messiah Jesus. They took her pain upon themselves and entered into her world. In a small church she heard the message that gave her the peace that had eluded her for her whole life. She realized her sin and her need for the blood atonement of Messiah Yeshua- Jesus. She hung onto Romans 10:9 which says, "If thou shall confess with thy mouth the Lord Jesus the Messiah and shall believe in thy heart that our Heavenly Father has raised Him from the dead, thou shall be saved." She realized that Messiah Yeshua- Jesus was her blood atonement, and she repented of her sin and asked Him into her heart and life.

It was then that she knew that her name was surely written in the book of life. She was filled with absolute peace and joy. She was a new creation, and her joy overflowed to all around her. Within six months time, her mother also came to Messiah. Frances remains a vibrant believer, always giving thanks to the L-rd our G-d for that small church where people entered the tents of Shem to bring a lost Jewish lady home to her Lord.

We must remind Israel that our Father Himself has said that blood is needed for the remission of sin; it is the blood that makes atonement for the soul (Lev. 17:11 and Talmud Yoma 5a). We must tell all people that there is none that does good; every one of us is unclean; we are all impure (Ps. 53:2-4). There is not a just man upon earth that does good and sins not (Ecc. 7: 20).

We celebrate this holiday by testifying that the L-rd our G-d has started a new creation, not just a new year. He was, is now, and always will be, faithful to His promises. We cry out with the apostle in Ephesians 5:14: "Awake you that sleep and rise from the dead and Messiah shall give you the light."

The L-rd our G-d requires us to be holy just as He is holy (Lev. 11:44). Ezekiel 18:20 tells us that the soul that sins will die. Ezekiel 33:11 adds that our Father has no pleasure in the death of the wicked, but would rather that the wicked turn from his way and live. Proverbs 20:9 asks, "Who can say, I have made my heart clean, I am pure from my sin?"

Scripture tells you to call on the name of Yeshua the Messiah and you will be saved from eternal punishment. Now is the time to call upon Him; now is the time for newness of life. Now is the time to believe and put your faith and trust in the only sacrifice that is acceptable to the L-rd our G-d. Believe on Yeshua the Messiah and you will be saved. Commit yourself to Him, and He will bear all your sins.

Yom Kippur

INTRODUCTION:

Yom Kippur is the holiest day of the Jewish year. It is the Day of Atonement, the Day of Judgment, the Sabbath of Sabbaths. It is a convocation involving a kippah, or covering, for sin. On this day two goats were sacrificed; one was killed as a sacrifice for sin, and the other one carried Israel's sins away into the wilderness. These two lambs were a single sacrifice, a type of the sacrifice of Messiah Yeshua, who was sacrificed on Calvary's cross and paid for the sins of all who would come to Him.

The Law of Moses offered forgiveness from sin to those people who sinned unintentionally. Starting with Leviticus 4:1 Scripture lists these people according to different categories - an anointed priest (4:3ff.), the entire Israelite community (4:13ff.), an individual leader (4:22ff.), and an individual member of the community (4:27ff.). The law of forgiveness covered not only the sins of commission but also of omission - failure to do one's civic duty (5:1), failure to regard the Lord's holy things (5:14ff.), and the violation of a trust (6:1ff.). These are classified as sins that require a guilt offering because the one who has committed them has been guilty of wrongdoing not only against his neighbor but also against our L-rd our G-d (5:19). The Law of Moses was unable to offer forgiveness to anyone who sinned presumptuously or defiantly. That person was to be cut off from his people because he despised his Father's word. His guilt would remain upon him (Num. 15:30).

In practical terms this person would remain part of physical Israel, but he would be cut off from spiritual Israel. This mystery is explained in the New Covenant Scriptures in Romans 9:6ff where Paul writes that not all who are descended from Israel are Israel, nor are they Abraham's children because they are just his physical descendants. There is a spiritual Israel that follows the L-rd our G-d by faith, and there is another Israel that follows Him in the natural sense only. All the people of all times who have come to our L-rd and our G-d and followed Him by faith comprise the body of spiritual Israel. These people have walked on the narrow road and entered through the straight gate that leads to everlasting life (Luke 13:24 and Matthew 7:13, 14). The identification of spiritual Israel is a spiritual call. In most instances only our Father knows the truth. This idea is still applicable to us today. There are many who say that they are followers of Messiah, but it is obvious that their spirit does not bear witness with His Spirit that they are His children. They go through all the motions, but the truth is not in them. Again, identification of these people is a call only our Father can make; He is the only one who can look upon a man's heart to see whether it is defiant or broken. Scripture is teaching us that there is a people called Israel who is one with the Father spiritually, and a people that is still called Israel although she is not united spiritually to our Father.

Strangers and sojourners in the land were covered by the same laws that governed national Israel. If those aliens were unrighteous, then they were unrighteous Gentiles. But if they were righteous before our Father, then they belonged to spiritual Israel. In Romans 9:6 the Apostle Paul gives the definitive statement on this subject when he says that not all that are descended from Israel (the nation) are Israel (of the spirit).

Based on Numbers 15 and Romans 9, we can safely say that there is an Israel that is after the L-rd our G-d's Spirit and an Israel that is not. The Israel of the Spirit remains the people of our Father both on earth and in Heaven, while the other (although His people) will not see eternal life with Him in His heavenly kingdom. The people who had broken and contrite hearts and were His people on earth (and in His mind, in Heaven) were covered by the forgiveness typified on the Day of Atonement. Even though the scapegoat carried the nation's sins away only into the wilderness, our Fathers looked into the future work of Messiah; and the sins of the redeemed were forgiven on the basis of Messiah's future sacrifice.

In the history of the Jewish people there have been special periods of revival that have involved large contingencies of Jewish people, when the Spirit of our Father came down upon them and convicted them of their sin, while revealing Messiah Jesus to their hearts and minds.

John Duncan, who was both a missionary and a professor of Hebrew at New College, Edinburgh, Scotland in the nineteenth century, tells of such a time: "Our hands now became so full of work that frequently, we had not time so much as to eat bread; from early morning until late at night we were occupied guiding, counseling and instructing those who were inquiring earnestly what they must do to be saved.... for a time the whole Jewish community was deeply moved wondering where unto these things would grow." (The Life of John Duncan, by David Brown, page 334).

Dr. Israele Zolli was the former chief rabbi of Rome. He was born in Brody, Poland, in 1881. He studied Philology and Rabbinics in Vienna; and in 1910 he was elected rabbi in Trieste. At the end of World War I he was appointed chief rabbi of Trieste, which in that year was annexed to Italy. He taught Hebrew and Semitic languages at the University of Padua in Italy and published numerous studies on Jewish history and philology in distinguished periodicals. In 1939 he was elected chief rabbi of Rome.

Rabbi Zolli made the following remarks in 1959, in a magazine called The Mediator: "Is conversion an infidelity, an infidelity towards the faith previously professed? To answer hurriedly yes or no would not be just: too much zeal would be displayed one way or the other, and too much zeal is notoriously harmful. Before answering, one should stop and ask oneself what is faith? Faith is an adherence, not to tradition or family or tribe, or even a nation, it is an adherence of one's life and works to the will of our Heavenly Father as revealed to each in the intimacy of one's own conscience. Was Saul of Taurus unfaithful? How many Jews he cast into prison! How merciless he was against his brothers, who were guilty only of having accepted the message of Messiah Yeshua! Jews are becoming converts today, as in the days of Saul-Paul, and have much, or even all, to lose in regard to earthly life, and have much, if not all, to gain in the life of grace." Rabbi Dr. Zolli was a believer when he wrote the above about faith and conversion.

Dear reader, I would ask you this question: is your hope of eternal life based on your own accomplishments or is it based on the work of Messiah Yeshua? His works have been approved and accepted by the L-rd G-d, while yours have not and never will be.

THREE QUESTIONS AND THEIR ANSWERS

How was Yom Kippur established?

How was and is Yom Kippur celebrated?

What are the implications of Yom Kippur under the New Covenant?

How was Yom Kippur established?

Before there could be atonement for sins, there had to be shedding of blood. Moses tells us in Leviticus 17:11-12 "for the life of a creature is in the blood and I have given it to you to make atonement for yourselves on the altar; it is the blood that makes atonement for one's life. Therefore I say to the Israelites, 'None of you may eat blood, nor may an alien living among you eat blood.'"

Leviticus 23:27-32 records the L-rd G-d's instruction to Moses: "'The tenth day of this seventh month is the Day of Atonement. Hold a sacred assembly and deny yourselves and present an offering made to the L-rd our G-d by fire. Do no work on that day, because it is the Day of Atonement, when atonement is made for you before the L-rd our G-d. Anyone who does not deny himself on that day must be cut off from his people. I will destroy from among his people anyone who does any work on that day. You shall do no work at all. This is to be a lasting ordinance for the generations to come, wherever you live. It is a Sabbath of rest for you, and you must deny yourselves. From the evening of the ninth day of the month until the following evening you are to observe your Sabbath.'" Yom Kippur was to be celebrated from sundown (approximately 6 PM) of the ninth day, for twenty-four hours, until 6pm of the tenth day. Biblical Jewish time reckons the start of a day at sundown and its end twenty-four hours later.

The holidays in Judaism do not correspond exactly to the same days in the solar calendar every year, because Israel uses a lunar calendar that has twelve months with either twenty-nine or thirty days in each month. The addition of another month after a three-year period makes up the difference.

How was and is Yom Kippur celebrated?

Because this day was so solemn, the Israelites prepared for it in advance. The High Priest was separated from the rest of the people for seven days before the Day of Atonement. When he officiated on this day, he washed (immersed) his body five times and his feet ten times; and he dressed plainly, so that he would have nothing with which to boast. He had to remove his garments of glory-the breastplate, ephod, girdle, and robe with pomegranates and bells on the bottom. He put on white linen breeches and his white uniform with a simple head covering. White signified purity. Although he was the High Priest, on the outside he looked just like a regular priest, except that his head covering was a little more elaborate.

The High Priest was the only one who could enter the Holy of Holies, and then only on Yom Kippur. On this day, when the High Priest went in, he would sprinkle blood before the mercy seat, first for his sins and then for the sins of the people. The mercy seat covered the Ark of the Covenant, and the ark held the symbols of Israel's rebellion which were the second set of Ten Commandments, the pot of manna, and Aaron's rod that budded. The L-rd our G-d, by this mercy seat, showed that He would cover the symbols of Israel's rebellion with His mercy. The Pharisees, as well as modern rabbinic Judaism, tell us that the Day of Atonement was for Israel's corporate sins as a nation and not for the individual sins of the people. But the Scriptures tell us in Leviticus 16:30 that the Day of Atonement was made for the people-to cleanse themselves so that before their Father their King they would be clean from all their sins.

Today, the Jewish people live under a religious system called rabbinic Judaism. They do not believe that we are now living under the New Covenant or that the Old Covenant has passed away, never again to be enacted. They do not believe that the basic requirements for fulfilling our Father's law have been elevated to a higher standard.

Since the Temple was destroyed in A.D. 70, rabbinic Judaism has adapted the sacrificial laws to the changing conditions that the Jewish people have experienced. Rabbinic Judaism says they cannot offer a sacrifice for their sin because the Temple no longer exists. It says that they do not sacrifice animals any longer because blood is no longer needed for the remission of sin. For animal sacrifice it substitutes doing good works, giving to charity, studying, and praying. We should note that the law always required these deeds to be performed along with the animal sacrifice. These deeds demonstrated that a man had a broken and contrite heart, while the blood was needed for remission of sin. The problem with the rabbinic system is that it is not ordained by our Heavenly Father.

The rabbis point to Psalm 51:17 where David wrote, "a broken and contrite heart, O G-d, you will not despise." They say that because we no longer have a Temple in which to sacrifice, this is all that is now required. This makes our L-rd's provision for salvation null and void, and it supplants it with a man-made system of salvation based on man's accomplishments. They maintain that their good works and a twenty-four hour fast will satisfy our Father's requirements. They are wrong on three accounts:

David was most surely sacrificing at the Temple while he was repenting in his heart. If he had forgone the sacrifice at the Temple, the people of Israel would have been in an uproar. The L-rd our G-d would not have called him a man after His own heart who would fulfill all of His will (acts 13:22), nor would He have said that "David did that which was right in His eyes and turned not aside from any thing that He commanded him all the days of his life, save only in the matter of Uriah, the Hittite" (1 Kings 15:5).

In the same year that Messiah was sacrificed on Calvary's cross, our Heavenly Father removed His Shekinah Glory from the Temple, thereby making any sacrifice that was brought to the Temple to be of no value as far as salvation was concerned.

Isaiah 64:6 tells us: "All of us have become like one who is unclean, and all our righteous acts are like filthy rags; we all shrivel up like a leaf, and like the wind our sins sweep us away." This nullifies any works as a way to obtain salvation.

On the Day of Atonement, according to Leviticus 16:29, Israel is supposed to afflict her soul. The way Israel afflicts her soul is to deny herself by fasting for twenty-four hours. Modern rabbinic Judaism also teaches that during this holiday, man is to be reconciled with his fellow man as well as with the L-rd our G-d. Unhappily, it is attempting to make reconciliation with our Father by means of which it, but not our Father, approves. Its observance of this holiday has become legalistic. It is impossible for sinful mankind to keep this convocation.

The ultra-orthodox Jewish people say if just one Jewish man can keep the 613 laws of the Sabbath just one time, then Messiah will come. Israel has never been able to accomplish that feat in the past, and she will not be able to accomplish it now. Furthermore, if one sinful man can accomplish this feat, then any and all of mankind can accomplish it; therefore, there would have been no need for Messiah to come. There is only one way to Heaven, and that is through Y'shua the Messiah. John 14:6.

Man is not able to keep the laws of the Sabbath, regardless of how sincerely or avidly he tries. The Lord of the Sabbath, the One who Himself ordained the Sabbath, has completed the demands of the Sabbath, because He was the Word made flesh that came to dwell among us (John. 1:14).

The L-rd our G-d is interested not only in the abstinence from eating; He requires true fasting. Isaiah 58 is clear regarding the requirements for a fast. We are to loosen the chains of injustice, to set the oppressed free, to provide for the poor, to share our food with the hungry, and to provide clothes and a shelter for those who are naked. The L-rd our G-d said that when Israel did these things, He would hear her and bless her.

The sacrifice required on the Day of Atonement had to be repeated year after year, thus showing that it was not a permanent atonement. The only way atonement can be made permanent is through the death of Messiah (Hebrews 7:27; 9:28; 10:10-14). The fact is, not only the Holy Scriptures, but Jewish literature as well, proves the rabbinic position to be erroneous. The Talmud tells us, in Yoma 5a, that without the shedding of blood there is no remission of sin. In Yoma 39b and Rosh Hashanah 31b, it is recorded that the rabbis said that our Father's Shekinah glory departed from the Temple forty years (A.D. 30; the year Messiah was crucified) before it was destroyed in A.D. 70. This departure was made evident by four miracles.

First, the Temple doors were made of heavy Corinthian brass, and it took thirty Levites to open them. Now the doors of the Temple would open and close by themselves.

Second, the lot for the sacrificial goat always came up in the priest's left hand. From this time forward, it always came up in the priest's right hand, showing that our Father's glory was not in the sacrifice.

Third, the westernmost candle in the Temple menorah was always lit first and burned the longest. Now this candle would no longer burn continually, showing that our Father our King's special blessing was removed from it.

Fourth, it was the practice to tie a crimson strap to the horns of the scapegoat and also to the Temple door. The L-rd G-d always turned these straps white to show that He had forgiven Israel for her sins. From this time on, the straps never turned white, showing that He has not and does not forgive Israel for her sins.

Our Father's Spirit no longer resided in the Temple because at Shavuot (Pentecost) His Spirit entered the hearts of true believers, and there is where it will remain throughout this age. The reason Jewish people cannot sacrifice is not because they do not have a Temple. It is because our Father's glory departed from the Temple.

During the entire last forty years of the Temple's existence our Father never forgave Israel for her sins. This happened because our Father had provided His own sin bearer, who was Yeshua the Messiah. When Israel rejected Him, she had to bear her own sins, which she does to this day. It is exactly the same for the Gentiles; when they reject Messiah in this life, they bear their own sins to their own damnation.

A special prayer winds itself through the five Yom Kippur services held this day. It says: "For the sins we have committed against Thee under stress or through choice, in stubbornness or in error, in the evil meditations of the heart or by word-of-mouth, by abuse of power, by exploiting or dealing treacherously with our neighbor bear with us, pardon us, forgive us!"

The historic beginning of rabbinic Judaism occurred when Johanan Ben Zakki certified the four proofs that the glory of the Almighty One had departed from the Temple. Since Zakki did not believe on the Yeshua the Messiah, he substituted a works salvation for the grace salvation provided by our Eternal Father.

The Talmud tells us that on his deathbed Johanan Ben Zakki was in great turmoil because he had great fear as to his judgment. When he was taken ill, all his students came to visit him. When he saw them, he started to weep. His disciples asked him, "O light of Israel, Pillar of the Right Hand, Strong Hammer, why dost thou weep?" He replied, "Now I am to be led into the presence of the king of kings, the Holy One, Blessed be He, who lives, and is through all eternities, whose anger, if He is angry with me, is an eternal anger. If he fetters (binds) me, it will be with everlasting fetters and if he puts me to death, it will be an eternal death. I will not be able to appease him with words nor bribe him with money. There are only two ways open to me; the first will lead to Paradise and the second will lead to Gehenna (hell), and as I do not know upon which of these two ways I shall be led, shall I not weep?" His students assured him that the Almighty One would look kindly upon him because of the great things he had done. Nevertheless, he was still exceedingly fearful. After all the assurances he had given to Israel regarding forgiveness for sin, all he could say to his students was "Who can stand before the Almighty One-who knows how he will be judged?"

When our Father no longer turned the crimson cloth white, the rabbis made up their own system of forgiveness. Instead of leading the sin-bearing scapegoat into the wilderness, Israel killed the scapegoat in a non-ritualistic manner. The man who led the goat took him to a cliff ten miles from the city. There he tore the crimson cloth in two. One piece he left on the goat and the other piece he attached to a rock. After doing this, the goat was thrown off the precipice. The reasoning was that Israel's national sins died with the goat and did not exist anymore, which would make up for the fact that Elohim did not forgive them.

Josephus, the Jewish historian of the first century A.D., tells us that the priests were sacrificing to the L-rd G-d for Israel's sins when the Roman soldiers broke into the Temple in 70A.D. The Almighty One could not and would not acknowledge their sacrifice, because they were operating under a covenant that no longer existed.

I have a friend who was a missionary in Israel for many years. He told me about the ritual of Kapporot, which started in the ninth century, and about which I had only heard, but never seen. On the day before Yom Kippur, people would sacrifice for their sin. The father of the household would take a white rooster, swing it over his head three times, and say the following: "This is my substitute, my vicarious offering, my atonement. This animal shall meet death, but I shall find a long and pleasant life of peace." The father then does the same thing for all the members of his family. A rooster was used for males, and a hen was use for females.

In the religious section of Jerusalem, blood actually ran down the streets because of the number of chickens that were slaughtered. The L-rd our G-d, has never authorized the killing of chickens in His sacrificial system. The rabbis invented it to satisfy the consciences of the people, who knew they were sinful and needed a sacrifice to pay for their sin. The Jewish people have also used other systems to help pay for their sins. In times past, in Eastern Europe, Jewish people would inflict thirty-nine stripes upon themselves to pay for their sin. This was called Malkut.

Some rabbis quote Psalm 116:15, which reads, "Precious in the sight of the L-rd is the death of his saints." They say that this verse teaches that a person's death is a sacrifice for atonement. Some rabbis have said that when a person fasts, he is reducing his body mass and killing cells, which will help atone for his sins. Other rabbis claim that the death of Jewish people (i.e., the Holocaust) is their offering for the sins of Israel, as well as the Gentile nations.

Some people will pray at midnight during the month of Elul. This month immediately precedes the month in which the Feast of Trumpets, the Day of Atonement, and the Feast of Tabernacles occur. These prayers are known as the prayers for forgiveness.

On the night preceding Yom Kippur, there is a special service called Kol Nidre (all vows). The cantor usually recites this portion: "All vows, bonds, oaths, devotions, promises, penalties, and obligations: wherewith we have vowed, sworn, devoted and bound ourselves: from this Day of Atonement unto the next Day of Atonement, may it come unto us for good: lo all these, we repent us in them. They shall be absolved, released, annulled, made void, and of non effect: they shall not be binding nor shall they have any power. Our vows shall not be our vows; our bonds shall not be our bonds: and our oaths shall not be our oaths."

This is one of the most sacred services in Judaism today. The reason for this recitation is not because the Jewish people wish to get out of making any oaths; rather it is because they realize that there are many oaths that people make that they are unable to keep. In their minds, this also absolved the Jewish people of the vows they made when they were forcibly baptized into Christianity. They also may have vowed never to practice Judaism, to follow the Law of Moses, or two keep the Sabbath or any of the holidays ever again. Since they would not have meant those vows, they were absolved of them.

The rabbis have come up with many theories on how to pay for their sins; but as none of them are Scriptural, they, therefore, are unacceptable to our Heavenly Father.

One can feel the longing of the Jewish people to be cleansed, to be right with our Father who is our King. The Apostle Paul (the apostle to the Gentiles) tells us that their zealousness is not based on knowledge. He also tells us that he could wish that he were cut off from Messiah for the sake of those of his own race (Rom. 9:3). Paul is not alone in his desire for Israel; Messiah wept over Jerusalem's children (inhabitants) and longed to gather them as a mother hen gathers her chicks (Luke 13:34).

Israel as a nation is far from the salvation that she so eagerly desires. In the future, there will come a day when Israel will look upon Him who was pierced and mourn for Him as one mourns for an only son (Zachariah 12:10) Y'shua the Messiah is that person upon whom they will look. He was sinless and did not have to sacrifice for His own sin; yet He was sacrificed on Calvary's cross for His redeemed people. To Him belongs all the glory.

What are the implications of Yom Kippur under the New Covenant?

The Lord Messiah is both the maker and the substance of our atonement. Hebrews 2:17 tells us that He is the High Priest that makes reconciliation (atonement) for the sins of the people. He is the only one who is both fit for this work and worthy of this honor.

Before the service on Yom Kippur, the High Priest had to bathe himself and put on clean white linen garments that could never be worn again. All of this ritual points to the purity of Y'shua the Messiah. The High Priest could only go into the Holy of Holies by Himself (Lev. 16:17). The Lord Messiah also had to act by Himself. We are told in Isaiah 63:3, "He alone was to tread the winepress." Messiah was appointed by His Father to accomplish the work His Father had prepared for Him to do. John 17:4-9 records Messiah's own words, telling us that He undertook this job and that He prays for those His Father gave Him.

It was part of the Father's plan that all of the disciples forsook Messiah and fled. If any of His own were crucified with Him, it would look as if they assisted in the atonement. The Scripture is clear; the sacrifice of Messiah alone could atone for a person's sin.

Leviticus 16:33 tells us that the High Priest made atonement for the holy sanctuary, for the tabernacle, for the altar, for the priests, and for all the people of the community. This had to be repeated every year. Our atonement under the Jewish New Covenant is complete in Messiah and never has to be repeated again.

Aaron had to offer sacrifice for his own sin first and then for the sin of the people. He made his confession on the head of his sin offering. Our Lord Yeshua had no sin for which to answer. Hebrews 7:26 says, "such a great High Priest meets our need-one who is holy, blameless, pure, set apart for sinners, exalted above the heavens."

When Yeshua was baptized by John in the Jordan River, He did not stay there along with others who were confessing their sins (Matt. 3:6). Matthew 3:16-17 tells us, "As soon as Yeshua was baptized, He went up out of the water. At that moment heaven was opened . . . and a voice from heaven said 'This is my Son, whom I love; with Him I am well pleased.'" Yeshua went right out of the water because he had no sin to confess. He was sinless, and His Father commended Him.

The work of Yeshua, and that work alone, gives us access to God the Father. Yeshua was not only the final sacrifice for sin; He was in reality the only sacrifice that could pay completely for sin. The book of Hebrews makes it perfectly clear that all the blood of all the bulls and all the goats slaughtered under the Old Covenant could never take away sin (Heb. 10:4). All that the animal blood could do was to cover (or kippur) the sin until the time that Messiah came to take it away.

Messiah was actually prefigured by the two goats sacrificed on Yom Kippur. These two goats were considered to be one offering. The slain goat was a type of Messiah, dying for our sins; and the scapegoat was a type of Messiah, carrying away our sins. The principle has never varied; before man's sins can be taken away, they must be paid for by the shedding of blood. This procedure was always followed by Israel. Our Father's lamb was slain before the scapegoat was led away to the wilderness with Israel's sins. The Scripture tells us that Messiah was delivered by the determinant counsel and foreknowledge of G-d (Acts 2:23). The L-rd our G-d supplied the goats to cover man's sin, as well as providing Messiah to take away man's sin.

Isaiah 53:6 says that Messiah bore the iniquity of us all. I Peter 2:24 says that He bore our sins in His own body upon a tree. The Father made Messiah, who had no sin, to be sin for us, so that in Him (Messiah), we might become the righteousness of G-d (2 Cor. 5:21). The sacrifice of Messiah occurred once, and then it was done. It was one time for all time.

When an individual becomes a new creation in Messiah Yeshua, that individual is seated with Him in the heavenly realms (Eph 2:6). Even the blood of the sacrifice that the priests brought into the Holy of Holies could never clear the conscience of the worshippers (Heb. 9:9). On the other hand, the pure blood of Messiah both cleansed the conscience and obtained eternal redemption for all those who believe (Heb. 9:12, 14).

The perfect sacrifice of Messiah, who was unblemished, was able to cleanse our consciences from acts that led to death (Heb. 9:14). Hebrews 10:20 says we enter "by a new and living way opened for us through the curtain, that is, His body." Not only do we enter through a new and living way, but we also have an advocate before the Father, Messiah Yeshua the righteous. Our salvation is secure because of the sacrifice of our Bridegroom.

Because Yeshua has paid the price for our sin, all true believers are bidden to come into our Father's presence. The High Priest of Israel could not tarry in the holy place, but our High Priest sits in the heavenly holy place, ever to intercede on behalf of His redeemed people.

Second Corinthians 5:21 tells us: "our Father made him who had no sin to be sin for us, so that in him we might become the righteousness of our Father." That which Messiah has paid, G-d will not charge to our account. Our sins are removed from us as far as the east is from the west, never to be remembered anymore (Ps. 103:12).

Not only are we as believers told to come into our Father's presence, but we are also told to come boldly before His throne. We have instant access to our Heavenly Father. When the High Priest went into the holy place, he had to burn incense before him. We are told Messiah is a sweet smelling savor to our Father, much better than mere incense. When we as believers confess our sin, the L-rd our G-d is faithful and just to forgive us our sins, based on the sacrifice of Messiah (1 John 1: 9). This will go on until one day when He will wipe the tears from our crying eyes with His pierced hands. It is then that we will see our Bridegroom face to face and enjoy His glory for eternity.

In Hebrews 9:11-14 we read, "But Messiah being come an high priest of good things to come, by a greater and more perfect tabernacle, not made with hands, that is to say, not of this building; neither by the blood of goats and calves, but by His own blood He entered in once into the holy place, having obtained eternal redemption for us. For if the blood of bulls and of goats, and the ashes of a heifer sprinkling the unclean, sanctified to the purifying of the flesh; how much more shall the blood of Messiah who through the eternal Spirit offered Himself without spot to our Father, purge your conscience from dead works to serve our G-d"

Rabbi Dr. Leopold Cohn is a fine example of one who, in our Father's grace, was turned from dead works to serve our living Father. Leopold was born in a little town in the eastern part of Hungary in the 1800s and was orphaned at the age of seven. Because he had to shift for himself, there were many days of terrible loneliness and bitter struggle just to exist. These days taught him to trust his heavenly Father with all his heart.

After his Bar Mitzvah at age thirteen, he was determined to become a rabbi and leader among his people. At eighteen, he had graduated from the talmudic academy with excellent scholarship and commendations as a worthy teacher of the law. He married a woman from a wealthy family, became ordained, and devoted himself to further study of the sacred writings. As was the custom in that area, he moved into the home of his in-laws. Rabbi Cohn had a burning desire to understand the exile from Israel and the delayed redemption that would come through Messiah.

Each morning he recited the twelfth article of the Jewish creed which declares, "I believe with a perfect faith in the coming of the Messiah, and though He tarry, yet I will wait daily for His coming." This started a flame in his heart as he looked for the fulfillment of our heavenly Father's promises of the restoration of scattered Israel. He no longer prayed the formal prayers of Judaism, but would rise up in the middle of the night to implore our Father to hasten the coming of the deliverer.

Rabbi Cohn started an earnest study of the original predictions of the prophets, albeit with great fear, because the Talmud curses the bones of one who calculates the timing of the end. Even though he was afraid that he would be struck by a bolt from heaven, he began to study the book of the prophet Daniel.

When he came to Chapter 9, he was electrified as he realized that the revered doctors of the law had covered up the truth by their commentaries. Verse 24 told him that Messiah should have come four-hundred years after Daniel received the prophecy of the seventy weeks from the divine messenger. It was not long before he started to question the reliability of the Talmud.

Rabbi Cohn was becoming very popular in the Jewish community as a teacher, and yet he felt in his own mind that he might be heretical. He was teaching from the Talmud, which he no longer trusted. He asked himself, "Should I believe the word of G-d, or must I shut my eyes to the truth?" It was at this point that he first started to pray a prayer that would stay with him for the rest of his life. He prayed "Open thou my eyes, O Father, that I may behold wondrous things in thy law."

During one of his sermons, his inner man with its many disturbing questions broke forth without control. His congregation loudly protested, and the service broke up with the people in an uproar. After that, Rabbi Cohn traveled a great distance to talk to a learned, aged rabbi for whom he had great respect. After he had unburdened his soul to the senior rabbi, the rabbi poured a stream of insults upon him that was impossible to bear. He accused him of being an upstart and of not having respect for the masters who knew all the intricacies of the law. The senior rabbi told him that if he did not change his ways, he would probably wind up among the apostates in America.

Rabbi Cohn latched on to the word America and became determined to go there. A short time later he and his family immigrated to Scotland. He left his family there with friends and continued on to New York City. In New York he was welcomed by his former countrymen who had immigrated there some years earlier. Since he was very famous in Hungary, the local rabbinic council immediately started to look for a congregation for him to lead.

One Sabbath afternoon, as he was taking a stroll, he saw a sign written in Hebrew in front of a building, saying, "Meetings for Jews." He did not know what to make of it; here was a church building with a cross on it, holding a meeting for Jews.

He was going to enter, and then someone he knew warned him against it saying, "There are apostate Jews in there and they are teaching that Messiah has already come." The rabbi turned away, waited a few minutes, and then went into the building. He wondered if these were the people about whom the senior rabbi in Hungary had spoken.

Immediately upon his entrance into the building, he fell into a state of shock. The speaker and every other person in the congregation were there without a head covering. To an Orthodox Jew this was the height of sacrilege. On the way out, he explained to the sexton his reason for leaving; and the sexton suggested that, since he could not stay for the service, perhaps he could call the minister for a private interview at his home.

Rabbi Cohn went to see the minister that following Monday morning and learned that not only was the minister a trained Talmudist; but he was also the scion of a famous rabbinic family. After they had spoken awhile, Rabbi Cohn told the minister about his messianic quest. The minister gave Rabbi Cohn a copy of the New Testament in Hebrew and asked him to study it.

Leopold arrived back in his room, opened the book, and saw the lines that would change his life forever. They were from the beginning of the book of Matthew: "This is the book of the generation of Yeshua the Messiah, the son of David, the son of Abraham."

His mind and his body were transformed immediately. It seemed to him that all of the physical and financial sacrifices he had previously made amounted to nothing. His endless hours of agonizing prayer were now about to receive their reward. He believed that the book came to him by the will of heaven and that his Heavenly Father had finally answered his prayers and would help him find the truth about Messiah.

He started to read the scriptures at 11 o'clock in the morning and did not stop until one hour after midnight. His joy was boundless; for he realized that Messiah's name was Yeshua, that He was born in Bethlehem, and that He came exactly at the time Daniel had predicted.

When he tried to share his news with other rabbis, he was told that he was crazy and that the Messiah he was talking about was actually Jesus of the Gentiles. He wondered to himself, "Can Yeshua the Messiah, the son of David, actually be Jesus whom the Gentiles worship?" He felt that if he were to believe in Jesus, he would commit rank idolatry.

As he read the Isaiah 53, prophetic vision of the suffering Messiah began to penetrate his mind. He wondered to himself, "How can I love the hated one and how can I defile my lips by repeating his name? How can I love him when his followers have tortured and killed my people through many generations? How can I join a community of people who hate my flesh and blood?" During all this anguish, there was still a small voice inside that said to him, "No matter what others have done in his name you must follow him, for He is Messiah."

He decided that he would devote himself to prayer and fasting until his heavenly Father clearly revealed to him what to do. As he was praying, his Hebrew Scriptures fell from his hands to the floor. When he bent down to pick it up his eyes fell upon the prophecy in Malachi 3.

"Behold, I will send my messenger, and he shall prepare the way before me, and the one whom ye seek, shall suddenly come to His temple, even the messenger of the covenant, whom you delight in: behold He shall come, saith the King of hosts" (v.1). Immediately Leopold Cohn fell to his knees and confessed Yeshua as Messiah and vowed to serve Him no matter what the cost. In that hour he knew that he had become a new creature in Messiah.

When he started to proclaim this fact to all his friends and acquaintances, they told him that he was mentally confused because he was away from his loved ones. When he continued his proclamations, he was branded as a traitor to his people and was persecuted bitterly. Members of the community wrote to his wife about his apostasy, and immediately she stopped communicating with him.

His life was in terrible danger in New York. The Hebrew Christian minister who had given him his first New Testament learned about his plight and, along with a group of friends, gave him shelter and protection. They made arrangements for his departure to Scotland where he could meet with his family and continue his studies. Leopold found a cordial welcome among the people of the Barkley church in Edinburgh, where he had made arrangements to be baptized. He knew that the army of Satan would be in battle formation against him. Once he made an open confession of his faith in Messiah, he would be in danger of losing his wife, children, friends, and all he held dear.

He had been in great turmoil up to the morning of his baptism, when he suddenly felt strengthened and cheery. All his problems were dispelled by the presence of his Messiah whom he was so eager to confess. Later on, he found out through correspondence with others that there was a large group of people who had been praying for him, including Dr. Andrew A. Bonar, the venerable pastor of Finnieston church in Glasgow. Leopold was no longer a rabbi of the law; he was now a messenger of his Messiah.

His wife and his children came to faith, and they all returned to New York where he founded the American Board of Missions to the Jews, later renamed Chosen People Ministries. The Jewish community looked upon him with hostile eyes, while Christians who should have rallied to his help did not.

Heartbreaking days lay ahead; his wife sold all the jewelry and other treasures that were given to her by her family so that they could pay the rent for their humble meeting hall. Their children went to school half-fed, but the family's spirits would not be broken. They had trusted themselves to the Messiah of Israel who would never forsake them.

One day as he was sharing Messiah, he was beaten to a pulp. With his typical humility he said that a servant should not expect better treatment than his master. Dr. Cohn continued to preach and teach.

Eventually there arose a large congregation to which he ministered. In 1930, when there were a great number of fierce attacks against him, Wheaton College conferred upon him an honorary Doctor of Divinity degree.

He passed away in 1937. His service was conducted at the Marcy Avenue Baptist Church in Brooklyn, New York, by the Ministerial Association of Brooklyn. Many, many pastors and laymen testified favorably about this valiant soldier of the cross. He was a true gift to the church, an undershepherd who had a passion for souls. His work for the glory of his Master had stretched to almost all quarters of the globe.

It was said about him that he had fought a good fight, finished his course, and kept the faith. Henceforth, there is laid up that crown of righteousness, which the L-rd our G-d, the righteous judge, will give him, and not to him only, but to all those that love his appearing. Those who knew him will remember him best for his humility of spirit. He always preached about redemption in the blood of the lamb, Yeshua the Messiah. Like Moses, the great emancipator of Israel, Dr. Cohn knew not that his face was aglow after talking with his Father. Therein lay his greatness.

CONCLUSION

When we celebrate this holiday, we give Messiah glory for his sacrifice. We are in Him, and we will be with Him forever in His heavenly kingdom.

While the Jewish people had to wait from year to year to see if they had redemption, the believer has obtained eternal redemption through Yeshua the Messiah. At this time, Jewish people have no temple, no priesthood, no altar for atoning sacrifice, and no forgiveness for sin.

For a sacrifice to be efficacious, it has to be acceptable to the L-rd our G-d. The Scripture says that without the shedding of blood there is no remission of sin (Lev. 17:11). When talking about sin, King David said "a broken and contrite heart, thou will not refuse" (Ps. 51:17).

Rabbinic Judaism teaches that a broken and contrite heart will pay for sin. But we must remember that, while King David said this, he was sacrificing for his sin. Both a broken and contrite heart and the blood sacrifice were required in Old Covenant times and both are needed for the removal of our sin under the New Covenant as well.

Most people of Israel have had their eyes shut and their ears made heavy (Is. 6:10). At this time, only a remnant is coming to Messiah (fourteen percent according to the Federation of Jewish Federations). Zechariah tells us that there will be a time when two thirds will be destroyed and one-third will be refined as coming through fire. It is then that the remainder will call on Messiah, and He says that He will hear them.

The Scripture is clear; all have sinned and come short of the glory of G-d. There is none righteous, no not one. Today, Messiah is building His church and His words are clear: "'Come to me all you who are weary and burdened, and I will give you rest. Take my yoke upon you and learn from me; for I am gentle and humble in heart, and you will find rest for your souls. For my yoke is easy and my burden is light" (Matt. 11:28ff.).

This is the message we are to bring to the Jew first and then to the Greek (Rom. 1:16). The Gentiles are not to be high-minded, for the L-rd our G-d can break them off the tree of salvation just as He did Israel (Rom. 11:13-21).

If you say that Yeshua is your Savior, I have a question for you. Do you weep over Jerusalem just as your Prophet, Priest, and King did? If you do not, then my next question is why not? Are you one of those who say that He is a believer in Messiah and only want Him to bear your burdens without your bearing His? If that is true, shame on you. You are missing one of His most vibrant blessings.

If you are a believer, our Father who is our G-d has some promises for you regarding your sin.

He will remember it no more (Heb. 8:12).

He will cast it behind His back (Is. 38:17).

He will tread it under foot and cast it into the depths of the sea (Micah 7:19).

He has removed your transgressions from you as far as the east is from the west (Ps. 103:12).

I invite you to think about your sin and what it cost Messiah to pay for it. If you are covered by the blood and righteousness of Messiah Yeshua, you can confess your sins and you will be forgiven (1 John. 1:9).

The Shofar that blew every fifty years on Yom Kippur announced the Jubilee (Ex. 25: 9-10). Come to Yeshua , now and make this your year of Jubilee. Start your life anew, and reap blessings while on this earth as well as for eternity in heaven.

If you have not committed yourself to Messiah and your spirit does not bear witness with His spirit that you are His child, I invite you to come to Him now. To obtain salvation, you need a kinsman redeemer; you need the mediator of the New Covenant (Heb 8:6; 12:24). You need Yeshua the righteous, the King of Glory. Repent of your sin, believe on the Lord Yeshua the Messiah, and you will receive His salvation.

Sukkot: The Feast of Tabernacles

INTRODUCTION

Sukkot is the seventh special Levitical feast. It occurs in the seventh month and is celebrated for seven days. In the Scriptures, seven is the number of completion, while three is the number of royalty or majesty. This seventh feast is celebrated in the seventh month for seven days. Three sevens indicate the royal completion of all things. This was the last time during the lunar year that the L-rd our G-d required the males of Israel to appear before Him. He had said that no man should appear before him empty-handed; each man had to bring a gift in proportion to the way our Father had blessed him (Deut.16:16ff).

This festival was a time for rejoicing. The L-rd our G-d wanted the people not only to rejoice, but He also wanted them to remember that He always had been faithful to His word. Every seventh year (in the year of the cancellation of debts), at the feast of Tabernacles our Father's law was to be read before all the people, including the aliens living in the land (Deut.31:9ff.).

The final rejoicing for the Jewish people will be when they come to look upon the face of the One who died for their sin. In his message "To the Jew First" Robert Murray McCheyne said, "Converted Israel will give life to the dead world. Just as we have found among the parched hills of Judah, that the evening dew, coming silently down, gives life to every plant, making the grass to spring and the flowers to put forth their sweetest fragrance, so shall converted Israel be when they come as dew upon a dead, dry world. The remnant of Jacob shall be in the midst of many people as a dew from our Father, as the showers upon the grass, that tarrieth not for man, nor waiteth for the sons of man (Micah 5:7" [From: Memoir and Remains of R.M. McCheyne, by Andrew Bonar (reprint, Banner of Truth, 1966), page 489.]) In 1840 McCheyne went to Ulster to plead for the interest of the Jewish people. This stirred up great interest. The following year the Irish assembly resolved to establish a work among the Jewish people, and it established missions in Syria and Germany, believing "missionary enterprise is one of the means to bring about the restoration of Israel in accordance with the Scriptures." (Minutes of the General Assembly 1840-1850.)

Sukkot: The Feast of Tabernacles

THREE QUESTIONS AND THEIR ANSWERS

How was the Feast of Tabernacles established?

How was and is the Feast of Tabernacles celebrated?

What are the implications of this holiday under the New Covenant?

How was the Feast of Tabernacles established?

The Jewish Scriptures established the Feast of Tabernacles in Leviticus 23:33ff and Nehemiah 8:15b: The L-rd said to Moses, "Say to the Israelites: 'On the fifteenth day of the seventh month the Feast of Tabernacles begins, and it lasts for seven days. The first day is a sacred assembly; do no regular work. For seven days, present offerings made to the L-rd by fire, and on the eighth day hold a sacred assembly and present an offering made to the L-rd by fire. It is the closing assembly; do no regular work. . . On the first day you are to take choice fruit from the trees, and palm fronds, leafy branches and poplars, and rejoice before the L-rd your G-d for seven days. Celebrate this as a festival to the L-rd for seven days each year. This is to be a lasting ordinance for the generations to come; celebrate it in the seventh month. Live in booths for seven days: All native-born Israelites are to live in booths so your descendants will know that I had the Israelites live in booths when I brought them out of Egypt. I am the L-rd your G-d.'" (Lev. 23:33-36, 40-43).

"'Go out into the hill country and bring back branches from olive and wild olive trees, and from myrtles, palms, and shade trees to make booths'-as it is written" Neh. 8:15b

How was and is the Feast of Tabernacles celebrated?

During the month of Tishri, Jerusalem must have been a wonder to behold. It has been estimated that more than a million worshipers came to Jerusalem to celebrate the fall feasts. Many guests who were there for the festivals were accommodated in private homes. To advertise that they provided room and board, homeowners would put a table with a place setting in front of their home. Sometimes the visitors would sleep in the house, and sometimes they would sleep on the roof under a cloth canopy.

The entire city was alive with excitement for the twenty-three days that comprise the period from the Feast of Trumpets through the

Sukkot: The Feast of Tabernacles 139

end of the Feast of Tabernacles. According to the law the Israelites were required to appear at the Temple only for the Feast of Tabernacles and not for Trumpets or the Day of Atonement. However, many people came to celebrate the three festivals together.

The visitors that did not stay in private homes camped out in the surrounding countryside and on the Mount of Olives. Some worshipers built lean-tos and stayed in them the entire time they were in Jerusalem. Other worshipers just came into the city to celebrate the Feast of Tabernacles.

The whole countryside was dotted with small booths so that people could celebrate the holiday in Biblical fashion. During the Levitical feast days there were more than five-hundred priests officiating in the Temple. Alfred Edersheim tells us what it was like: "On the day before the Feast of Tabernacles, the fourteenth of Tishri, the Festival pilgrims had all arrived in Jerusalem. The booths on the roofs, in the courtyards, in the streets and squares, as well as roads and gardens within a Sabbath day's journey must have given the city and neighborhood an unusually picturesque appearance. The preparation of all that was needed for the festival would totally take up the worshiper's time. The purifications, the care of the offerings as well as friendly conversations would keep the worshippers busy. When the early autumn evening set in, the blast of the Priests' trumpets on the Temple mount announced to Israel the advent of the feast." (From: The Temple-- Its Ministry and Services)

The Talmud provides a description of the ceremony of the drawing of water. This was a very important ceremony to be performed during this Festival. There was always much pomp and circumstance with much exaggeration of ceremonies to give the L-rd our G-d all the glory. The people also chanted the words of Isaiah 12. There we read, "Behold Messiah is my salvation" and "make known among the nations what He has done, and proclaim that His name is exalted." The worshipers were to shout aloud and sing for joy for the greatness of the Holy One of Israel.

Water was significant, because Israel was an agricultural country and because there was always a need for moisture for the crops. This water-pouring ceremony was created by the Israelites to call upon their Creator to provide rain for their fields. All the crops had been harvested, and the people wanted water so that the ground would be in good condition for the seed that would be planted next year.

During the ceremony a priest descended the stairs from the Temple to the pool of Siloam. Accompanying him were worshippers and flutists. The priest filled a special gold pitcher with water and then started back to the Temple altar area. He returned through a gate that was called the Water Gate. As he stepped through the gate, he was greeted by a blast of the trumpet, which was similar to the shofar. There was one long blast, a quivering note, and then another long blast.

The priest went up the ramp to the southwest side of the altar. On the edge of the altar there were two magnificent silver bowls. A bowl with a wide mouth held the wine of the drink offering; and the other one, with a narrow mouth, was for the water from the gold pitcher. Once the water was in the bowl, the priest would spill both bowls onto the altar.

While the priest was pouring out the water, the flutists played and the choir sang Psalm 118 ("O Father Do Save, We Beseech Thee Our Father, We Beseech Thee, Do Send Prosperity"). While this was going on, the worshipers shook their palm branches toward the altar.

The water represented rain, and rain was symbolic of the Holy Spirit. The entire ceremony represented the day when the L-rd would "rain" His Holy Spirit on Israel (Joel 2:28, 29). There is no way to describe the joy of the participants during this Festival. Both the priests and the worshipers were excited to a high fever pitch.

John 7:37ff. Tells us: "On the last and greatest day of the Feast, Yeshua- Jesus stood and said in a loud voice, 'If anyone is thirsty, let him come to Me and drink. Whoever believes in Me, as the Scripture has said, streams of living water will flow from within him.' By this, He meant the Spirit, whom those who believed in Him were later to receive. Up to that time the Spirit had not been given, since Yeshua had not yet been glorified."

Yeshua used the setting of the water ceremony during the Feast of Tabernacles to offer the invitation: "Whosoever will, may come." In contrast to the water that is merely physical and must always be replenished, He offers the water that satisfies forever. In John 4:13, He calls for those who thirst after righteousness and promises to fill them with a spring of living water that wells up to eternal life. Isaiah the prophet says in 44:3: "For I will pour water on Him who is thirsty, and floods on the dry ground; I will pour My Spirit on your descendants and my blessing on your offspring".. The prophet Hosea wrote, "As surely as the sun rises, He will appear; He will come to us like the winter rains, like the spring rains that water the earth"

At the time described by John the nation was in a jubilant state. The people were looking eagerly for the promised Messiah, even though they only wanted Him to throw off the yoke of Rome. Yeshua was offering something far superior to liberation from political oppression; He would provide life eternal to all those who would come to Him.. He said, "I am the way, the truth, and the life." John 7:31 tells us that many believed on Him, and verse 43 records that the people were divided because of Yeshua.

The Talmud explains in Sukkah 5 that during this feast the Temple was gloriously illuminated. At the end of the first day of Tabernacles the priests and the Levites went down to the court of the women, where four enormous golden candlesticks were set. The candlesticks were fifty cubits high and had four golden bowls placed on them and four ladders resting against them. Four young men of priestly descent climbed the ladders and poured pure oil into each of the bowls.

The priests used their own worn-out liturgical clothing for wicks. The Talmud tells us that the light coming from these candelabra was so bright that there was no courtyard in Jerusalem that was not well lit. There was a festive atmosphere; and pious men and members of the Sanhedrin, along with leaders of the different religious schools, would dance well into the night, holding burning torches and singing songs of praise to our heavenly Father who is the King of Kings and L-rd of Lords.

The Levitical musicians played joyous music with harps, lyres, cymbals, trumpets, and other instruments. The musicians stood upon the fifteen steps leading down from the court of the Israelites into the women's court. These steps corresponded to the fifteen songs of ascent (Psalms 120–134).

These festivities continued long into the night. Two priests stood at the upper gate (Nicanor), which led down from the court of the Israelites to the court of the women. They held trumpets in their hands and waited for the signal, which was a cock's crow at dawn.

At the cock's crow they sounded the prolonged blast, a quivering note, and another prolonged blast on the Shofar; and they walked down the steps. They continued to blow their trumpets as they walked through the court of the women to the Beautiful Gate.

When they were through the gate, they turned to the west, facing the sanctuary in the Temple, and chanted the following prayer: "Our ancestors, when they were in this place, turned their backs unto the Temple and their faces toward the east, and they prostrated themselves eastward toward the sun; but as for us, our eyes are turned to the eternal." It was a magnificent ceremony, filled with beauty and symbolism, with light that represented the Glory of the L-rd that had filled the Temple.

In the brilliance of the gloriously illumined Temple, Yeshua cried out; "I am the light of the world. Whoever follows Me will never walk in darkness, but will have the light of life" (John 8:12).

This pronouncement of Yeshua caused yet another controversy with the Pharisees, who argued that Yeshua was simply elevating Himself and that, therefore, His witness was false. Ultimately, the Father who sent Yeshua bore witness of Him; and His testimony is true.

In this present age many Jewish people begin to build their Sukkahs (booths) immediately after sundown on the Day of Atonement. They do this with great expectation and with anticipation of the joy that comes with celebrating Tabernacles. Everyone in the family helps, and they decorate the booths beautifully.

The booths are built in a variety of places. Sometimes they are attached to the outside of a house; and other times they may be built in the yard, in the driveway, up on the roof, or on the fire escape of an apartment house. Rabbinic law states that they may never be built under a tree.

The Sukkah has only three constructed sides, with a curtain or drape hanging over the fourth side. The sides and the roof of the tabernacle are covered with olive and wild olive trees, myrtles, palms and shade trees. Enough space is left on the roof so that the inhabitants can see the stars and give our Father all glory. The Sukkah must be made as beautiful as it can be; so sometimes people put paintings in them. The Rabbis teach that the phrase in Exodus 15:2 ("the L-rd is my strength and my song; He has become my salvation. He is my G-d, and I will praise Him, my Father's G-d, and I will exalt Him.") refers to the booths of Sukkot. The Sukkah is open to all guests, rich and poor alike. During Sukkot in New York City, ultra-orthodox ride around in trucks that have booths built on the back of the trucks. They will park on the side of the road so that Jewish worshippers can come in to get something to eat and to pray.

Before the celebration of Tabernacles can begin, the celebrant must obtain the four species of plants that are to be waved before our Father. These wave offerings are called the lulav and etrog. The etrog is a citron, and the lulav has three species bound together-a palm branch in the center, three myrtle branches on the right, and two willow branches on the left situated a little lower than the myrtle branches. The celebrant holds the citron with the stem up in his left-hand and the lulav in his right hand and says the blessing. They are waved each morning in the Synagogue, except on the Sabbath.

There is a specific tradition as to how and why the lulav must be waved. It is waved three times facing the east, then the south, then the west, then the north, then above one's head, and then down to the floor. The four directions or to remind us of our Father to whom the four corners of the earth belong. The waving up and down is an acknowledgment of the L-rd our G-d who created Heaven and earth. It is done at specific times during the service, and then a blessing is said: "Blessed art thou O L-rd our G-d, King of the Universe, who has sanctified us by thy commandments and has commanded us concerning the waving of the lulav." When the family goes home and enters its Sukkah (booth), the father recites his blessing; and then all may eat.

Everyone sleeps in the Sukkah. If it rains, some say they may go inside; and some say they must stay outside for at least two hours. A favorite pastime is visiting among Sukkahs. The head of the house in the Sukkah says a prayer based on Deuteronomy 8:17-18, "Do not say in your heart by my own power and the might of my own hand have won this wealth for me. You should remember the L-rd, as it is He who gives you strength to make progress."

The people leave their houses that are full of every good thing at this season and dwell in booths as a reminder that there are people who have neither possessions nor houses in which to live. For this reason, the Holy One established the Feast of Tabernacles, so that none who celebrates the ingathering should be proud of his well-furnished home.

The last day of this festival is called The Hoshana Rabbah. It is very solemn as if it were a continuation of Yom Kippur. (Hoshana Rabbah literally means "the great salvation.") On all the other days of the Feast of Tabernacles the congregation circles the sanctuary one time, waving palm branches. On this day the congregation circles the sanctuary seven times in remembrance of the time that the children of Israel circled Jericho, and the walls fell down. Zechariah 4: 6 records our Father's reminder: "Not by might nor by power, but by my Spirit, says the King Almighty".

Shemini Atzeret is the eighth day of this festival. It is a Sabbath and a solemn assembly. These two holidays are joined together as one, but in reality they are two separate holidays. We will discuss this assembly in the next chapter.

On the Hoshana Rabbah Israel takes one last day to be alone with her L-rd. Families eat in the booth for the last time, and they make prayers for a good year and for rain. During this day the book of Ecclesiastes is read. In times past during the visitation among Sukkahs the learned men of the community would discuss Scripture.

When Solomon Ginsburg was fourteen years old (one year past his Bar Mitzvah), he was allowed to listen to the discussions of the learned men of Suwulki, Poland. These men came to debate Scripture in his father's Sukkah. As Solomon was listening to them, he was also fingering through their books that lay on the table. He picked up a well-worn copy of the prophets that opened to Isaiah 53. In the margin he noticed that someone had written, "To whom does the prophet refer in this chapter?" Without even thinking, he asked the men around the table that exact question. No one answered him, so he asked the question again; and, at that point, his father, who was a very famous rabbi, snatched the book out of his hand.

Solomon was not used to the rigidity of the Jewish community in Poland, because he had been reared in the home of his mother's parents in Koenigsberg, Germany. They were very liberal and had given him a liberal education. Now that he was back in Poland, his father wanted him to be a teacher and so arranged for him to be married to the daughter of a merchant who would support him while he studied the necessary seven years to become a teacher. At this point Solomon was only fifteen years old.

He left Poland and wandered around Europe for some time before finally finding his way to London, where he spoke to his mother's brother. His uncle took him into his home and gave him a job in his large dry goods store. One Sabbath, as he was taking a walk, he met a man who invited him to go to the Mildmay mission to hear an explanation of Isaiah 53. His mind immediately flashed back to the question he had asked at Sukkot in his father's home. He decided that he would go to listen to the lecture. That night, after listening to the exposition (a great part of which he did not understand), he decided to read the New Testament Scriptures. After struggling with his own spirit and the Spirit of the L-rd he was convinced that Yeshua-Jesus was indeed the Messiah of Israel. By faith, he came to his Messiah after listening to an exposition of Matthew 10:37 at the mission: "Anyone who loves his father or mother more than me is not worthy of me." He rose up and announced that he wanted to be worthy of Messiah.

As a result of his conversion he endured many trials with his uncle in London. Another uncle from Germany, plus many elders of Israel from Europe, went to England to convince him that he was wrong in his decision to follow Jesus as the Messiah of Israel.

He became a strong witness for Messiah while he spent three years learning the printer's trade and three years in Bible college. He received a call to go to Brazil, and he lived with a family in Portugal while learning the language. He became proficient in the Portuguese language, wrote a tract in English, translated it into Portuguese, had it printed, and sold three thousand copies. He used this money to help support himself. After becoming very proficient in the language, he immigrated to Brazil.

Because he was proclaiming the gospel, someone had put a price on his head. He suffered many trials and tribulations, but the Spirit of the L-rd constantly protected him from all his foes. He confronted the people who were paid to kill him. They repented and became strong followers of Messiah Jesus-Yeshua. They later became his protectors so that no one would harm him while he told the whole country of salvation in the Messiah and Savior Jesus. In simple words, he told the old story of our Father's love in Jesus the Messiah; that His redeeming power has been given to those who repent and forsake sin and turn to Him for full pardon.

He started many churches in various locations scattered over the hills and valleys throughout Brazil. These churches stood as a beacon in the midst of ignorance and superstition. He would start a church and stay there until it was large enough to have its own full-time pastor. When that was accomplished, he would move to another area and repeat the process. These churches then became centers of evangelism. Solomon used his printing skills and sent out a monthly bulletin called Good News to all the churches. The Southern Baptist Convention, with which Solomon Ginsburg was a missionary, said that he was decidedly the greatest missionary in Brazil.

What are the implications of this convocation under the New Covenant?

While it is true that the Feast of Tabernacles will have further fulfillment when all who comprise the bride of Messiah dwell with Him in Heaven, it is also true that this convocation has been completely fulfilled in Messiah as far as the redeemed on this earth are concerned. We are a new creation; old things have passed away; behold all things are become new (2 Corinthians 5:17). Our communication with Messiah is through His Spirit, for we have become a spiritual people.

The Feast of Tabernacles has direct application to every believer today. We are the Temple of our Father our King; we are victorious and glorious because Messiah completed all His work on this earth and rose to be with His Father. All believers have His peace, not as the world gives peace, but His peace and assurance of salvation.

We are safe, because He said He would neither leave us nor forsake us. We as believers must seek to dwell in the fullness of the Spirit each minute of every day of our lives. We truly can take the words from Isaiah 12, "behold my Creator is my salvation." These words should be the fruit of our lips that we share with the world as a testimony of the glory of Y'shua.

Messiah said in John 14:23, "If anyone loves me, he will obey my teaching. My Father will love him, and We will come to him and make Our home with him." If you are a believer today, then you are the Temple of the Holy Spirit. Let me ask you a question: is your Temple clean and in good condition? Does the Spirit of our Father find it a welcome place to dwell?

The Spirit brings with Him evidence of His occupancy. He makes our lives beautiful, just as Israel made her booths lovely. Does your life reflect the presence of our Father's Spirit? Does it show victory? Do you provide shade and nourishment for those who are in trouble? Are you a sweet savor unto them? Do you give our Father all the glory in your life? Does your light so shine before men that they see your good works and glorify your Father who is in Heaven (Matt. 5:16)? All of this is the result of the work of the Spirit as He lives in us and changes us to become more like our beloved Savior, Messiah Y'shua.

Our Father's word instructs us that the tabernacle or booth was to be made with branches from olive and wild olive trees, myrtles, palms, and shade trees. Messiah's bride would be composed of the natural olive tree and the wild olive tree. In essence, the bride is composed of both Jews and Gentiles. These redeemed people are to be a sweet smelling savor, just as myrtle leaves are sweet smelling. Messiah's bride would have victory in Him, just as the palm leaves are a symbol of victory. Messiah provided shade for the people of Israel as they wandered through the desert by the pillar of the cloud in the daytime and the pillar of fire at night. He provides spiritual shade for us under the New Covenant; and we, as His body, are to extend that concept to each other. As believers, we are to provide shade for one another as we travel this road toward the celestial city.

During the times of the Second Temple (Herod's temple, the one Yeshua knew), worshipers came into the temple area carrying torches during this holiday. In this context Messiah Yeshua said to the people, "You are the light of the world. A city on a hill cannot be hidden" (Matt. 5:14). We are to let our light so shine before men that they may see our good works, and glorify our Father who is in Heaven (Matt. 5:16).

Zechariah prophesied of a time when Jewish believers would flow out of Jerusalem and spread the gospel to the nations. In Zechariah 14:8, we read, "On that day living water will flow out from Jerusalem, half to the eastern sea and half to the western sea, in summer and in winter". That is just what happened as Jewish believers spread the gospel of Yeshua the Messiah among the nations. We, too, are to be that living water that flows over all the earth to spread the gospel of peace and salvation in Messiah Yeshua.

In our lives as believers we are to remember the mercy seat in the Tabernacle. The mercy seat was not cast, but it was beaten into shape using pure gold. When the mercy seat was finished, it was nothing like the raw material that was used to make it; but it was an object of great beauty. The finished product was well worked over for the glory of our L-rd.

How does this apply to you? Is your Heavenly Father beating you into shape for His glory? Are you fighting His training, or are you yielding to it? The Scripture clearly tells us that the Lord chastens those He loves. Yield to the L-rd and will make you a vessel of beauty.

John 7:37-39 tells us that in the last day of the great feast, Yeshua stood and cried, saying, "If any man thirst, let him come unto me and drink. He that believes on me, as the Scripture has said, out of his belly shall flow rivers of living water." Yeshua still offers the only water that satisfies.

Isaiah 44:3 says, "For I will pour water upon him that is thirsty and floods upon the dry ground; I will pour My Spirit upon thy seed and my blessings upon thy offspring." In Messiah Yeshua the blessing of salvation came to both the Jews and the Gentiles alike. Both received the promise of the Spirit through faith.

The prophet Zechariah spoke of a day when Israel and the nations will celebrate the Feast of Tabernacles (Zech. 14:16). At that time Israel will be redeemed, and her enemies will be destroyed. Before that happens, Israel will go through a period of great suffering. The prophet tells of Israel's agony during this terrible period. In Zechariah 13:8, 9 we read; "In the whole land,' declares the L-rd, 'two-thirds will be stuck down and perish; yet one-third will be left in it. This third I will bring into the fire; I will refine them like silver and test them like gold. They will call on my name and I will answer them; I will say, 'They are my people,' and they will say, the L-rd is our G-d.' "

These people will receive Yeshua's salvation. They will be assured of eternal life in Heaven with our Father. It is written in Revelation 21:3, 4 that our Creator Himself will be among His people and He shall wipe every tear from their eyes. There no longer shall be any death, mourning, crying or pain; for the old order of things will have passed away.

There will be a day when redeemed Israel will join a great multitude that will tabernacle (dwell) with the L-rd their G-d. In Revelation 7:9-10 we read, "After this I [John] looked and there before me was a great multitude that no one could count, from every nation, tribe, people and language, standing before the throne and in front of the Lamb. They were wearing white robes and were holding palm branches in their hands. And they cried out in a loud voice: 'Salvation belongs to our G-d, who sits on the throne, and to the Lamb.'"

Today there are many Jewish people who because of our heavenly Father's grace can now cry out, "Salvation belongs to our King who sits on the throne, and to the Lamb." Robert N. Perlis is one of them. He grew up in Reform Judaism, which teaches that the Bible could not possibly be literally true. It teaches that it is just a collection of history, stories, fables, and myths. To Robert, this did not seem enough of an explanation of the L-rd G-d, who seemed distant and cold. During his college years he searched for the answers to life's hard questions: Where did I come from? Why am I here? Do I have a purpose in this life? What happens after death? Is there a Heaven, and will I ever get there? Perlis spent many years searching for the answers in Hinduism, Zen Buddhism, and other similar religions; but none of these religions or philosophies could satisfy the emptiness deep inside of him.

All of these ideologies taught the same basic tenet: if one just works hard enough, he will be able to achieve enlightenment and be at peace with himself and with the universe. One can be in charge of his own destiny and become a sort of a god for himself. Perlis said to himself, "I don't think so! This cannot be. I am not responsible for my being here on this planet. I do not know when I am leaving, and I do not know where I am going." Robert decided to explore Judaism again, but at a much deeper level. He bought a Tanakh (the Jewish Bible, the Older Testament) and started studying.

A Christian friend pointed out some of the Messianic prophesies

(Jer. 31:31; Isa. 53; Ps. 22; Isa. 42; Dan. 9:26; and Zec. 12:10). Robert thought, "These sound like they are describing Jesus. I knew that Jesus was Jewish; nobody denied that, but was he the Messiah? Did we (Jews) miss him?" At this point, he was seeking truth. He was not focusing on "life questions;" he just was seeking truth. Either Jesus is the Messiah or he is not, true or false, real or a lie (a huge one at that, for His followers have numbered in the millions over the last two thousand years).

Robert decided to pray to the L-rd G-d and ask Him to reveal the truth. "Is Jesus the Messiah or not?" One night soon after studying some of these prophetic verses, he witnessed something amazing happening. Perlis knew with all his heart that Jesus (Yeshua) was the Messiah and that the Bible was completely true. The L-rd G-d had answered his prayer! His creator who was his Father and his King started a personal relationship with him. His Father had filled the emptiness in his heart with His Father's Spirit, and provided all the answers to Robert's questions in His letter to humankind, the Bible. Robert was finally home and finally understood what it meant to be Jewish. For the first time in His life, He was proud of that fact. His Father had chosen the Jews (Hebrews) through whom to reveal Himself; He entrusted them with His very words and it was through them that His Messiah came. Perlis realized that believing that Jesus was the Messiah was not a Gentile thing, but was completely Jewish.

He wondered how his people could have completely missed this. He later found out that many Jews had not missed it after all. Reading material from Jews for Jesus, the Messianic Jewish Alliance of America, and others, showed him that there were tens of thousands of Jewish believers all over the world; and that number was growing. With his new faith came a change in his attitude, philosophy and way of thinking. He felt convicted of sin in some of his old behavior and changed his mind on the liberal attitudes of his upbringing.

God was molding Robert and shaping him. Why not? After all, He is God! He is in charge, and Robert learned that he could completely trust Him, whether Robert knew what was going on or not. Wonderful, life-changing things happened to him after he knew and relied on Messiah Jesus. Messiah showed him his sins, cleansed him from them, freed him from them and lived in his heart. Messiah showed him time and time again that God's ways and path for Robert's life were perfect. Robert's testimony is that he knew he was eternally secure with Messiah. Robert confessed that he was glad that he was not in charge; he would have really messed up his life. He wondered if he were ever really in charge anyway?

CONCLUSION

In former times El-him provided booths for the children of Israel to dwell in during their forty years in the wilderness. He was always with them in the cloud by day and the pillar of fire by night. He took care of their physical as well as spiritual needs.

We who are redeemed are a new creation in Messiah; we are the resting place of G-d's Spirit. We are not of this world; we only reside in this world. As the booth in the past was decorated with all kinds of fruit, so we must exude the fruit of the spirit-love, joy, peace, long suffering, gentleness, goodness, faith, meekness, and temperance (Gal 5:22, 23a).

El-him's Word reminds us that we are His Sukkah in our present daily life. In addition, we are under His protection. We need Him each hour of every day. In Psalm 27:5 King David writes; "For in the day of trouble He will keep me safe in his dwelling [Hebrew Sukkah]; He will hide me in the shelter of His tabernacle and set me high upon a rock." We are not only protected in the tabernacle of Yeshua, but He has also set us upon a rock (Yeshua) and has told us that he will never leave us nor forsake us.

Our tabernacle in this life has the same qualities as the tabernacles of Israel. The thick branches were for shade and protection. The palm branches were an emblem of victory. The olive branches were for peace and plenty, and the myrtle was for a sweet smelling savor. Messiah Yeshua is all of this to us; as His body we are to imitate Him by exhibiting the same qualities.

There will come a time in the future when, in addition to our present indwelling by G-d's Spirit, we will dwell in a place that G-d created especially for those who are to be the bride of His Son. Ephesians 2 tells us that there is a sense in which we are already there, but in the future time we will be there experientially. As we celebrate this in the future, we will look back to see G-d's plan from eternity past and give Him the ultimate glory.

Holy, Holy, Holy is the Lord of Hosts. The whole earth is full of His glory. Remembering Tabernacles in the past and celebrating Tabernacles now help us look forward to that day when we will tabernacle with Him forever. And that will be the End!!!!

As the rain falls to nourish the crops, so the Spirit of G-d falls upon those who have identified with Yeshua in His death and resurrection. Jehovah says in Ezekiel 36:25; "I will sprinkle clean water on you, and you will be clean."

Let me ask you another question. What kind of a dwelling place for the Ruach Hakodesh (the Holy Spirit) are you? Does the Spirit find peace within you? Are you clean? Has G-d's Spirit come upon you to give you the new life in Him? Does your spirit bear witness with His Spirit that you are His child? If it does not, the Scripture is clear: believe on the L-rd Yeshua the Messiah, and you shall be saved.

The Talmud makes special reference to the seventy bullocks that were sacrificed during this holiday. It says that they were sacrificed for the sin of the seventy nations of the world. I submit to you the fact that in our day and age, the only sacrifice that would be efficacious for the sins of the world is the sacrifice of Messiah Yeshua the righteous. His sacrifice is sufficient to take away all the sins of all the people of all time. He is the only way to the Father. He is the only door through which mankind must enter to receive eternal life. It is required of every believer who is indwelt by the Spirit of the Almighty One to be involved in spreading that message. It is to be done in El-him's order: to the Jew first and then to the Gentile (Rom. 1:16).

Shemini Atzeret: The Eighth Assembly

INTRODUCTION

The book of Numbers spells out the fantastic number of sacrifices that were required at the Feast of Sukkot (Tabernacles) [Num. 29:12ff.]. During the weeklong celebration of the Feast of Tabernacles there were seventy bullocks sacrificed. The first day thirteen were sacrificed, and each successive day one less was sacrificed. On the seventh day the offering consisted of seven bullocks. In addition to the bullocks, fourteen rams and ninety-eight lambs were sacrificed.

The total number of all the animal sacrifices was 182. Along with each of the meat offerings there was an offering of three-tenths of an ephah of flour for the meal offering. These grain offerings totaled 336 tenths of ephahs of flour. The offerings, whether figured individually as a class, or grouped together, are divisible by seven. Seven evenly divides (182 = 7 x 26), as well as 336 (336 = 7 x 48). When we add the number of meat and meal sacrifices together, the total equals 518. Seven divides this number into groups of seventy-four (518 = 7 x 74). In the Scriptures seven is the number of completion. Two examples would be: 1) God's creating the heavens and the earth in seven days, included His rest, and 2) the number of days in the weekly cycle given to Israel.

The L-rd our G-d Himself decided on the length of all the convocations. He decided that the Feast of Tabernacles would be seven days in length and that following that festival there would be a one-day convocation that had to occur on the Sabbath. He gives us this as a picture of the new creation, which starts on the eighth day. Tabernacles signaled completion upon completion, and Shemini Atzeret signifies a new beginning. Israel as a nation could not look into the future and see what our L-rd's plan would be. The plan was that in the future there would be a time when all sacrificing would be completed, and a new creation would begin.

The following statement comes from The Works of Richard Sibbes, by A.B. Grosart. The Jews are not yet come in under Christ's banner; but our L-rd, that hath persuaded Japheth to come into the tents of Shem, will persuade Shem to come into the tents of Japheth (Genesis 9:27). The fullness of the Gentiles is not yet come in (Romans 11:25) . .

. But our Messiah Yeshua -Jesus will gather all the sheep His Father has given Him into one fold that there may be one sheepfold and one shepherd (John 10:16). The faithful Jews rejoiced to think of the calling of the Gentiles; and why should we not joy to think of the calling of the Jews? When the fullness of the Gentiles is come in, then comes the conversion of the Jews. Why may we not expect it? They were the special people of our Creator. We see Christ believed on in the world. We may, therefore, expect that they will also be called, there being many of them, and keeping their nation distinct from others." (Volume 1, page 99 and volume 5, page 517).

We will examine Shemini Atzeret by asking and answering three questions.

THREE QUESTIONS AND THEIR ANSWERS

How was Shemini Atzeret established?

How was and is Shemini Atzeret celebrated?

What are the implications of Shemini Atzeret under the New Covenant?

How was Shemini Atzeret established?

The Jewish Scriptures established Shemini Atzeret in Leviticus 23:36 and Numbers 29:35ff. Leviticus 23:36 states: "For seven days present offerings made to our L-rd by fire, and on the eighth day hold a sacred assembly and present another offering by fire. It is the closing assembly; do no regular work."

Numbers 29:35-38 adds: "On the eighth day hold an assembly and do no regular work. Present an offering made by fire as an aroma pleasing to the L-rd, a burnt offering of one bull, one ram and seven male lambs a year old, all without defect. With the bull, the ram and the lambs, prepare their grain offerings and drink offerings according to the number specified. Include one male goat as a sin offering, in addition to the regular burnt offering with its grain offering and drink offering."

How was and is Shemini Atzeret celebrated?

During this holiday there is a service in the morning at which someone offers a special prayer called Tefillat Geshem. This prayer is for

Shemini Atzeret: The Eighth Assembly   155

the dew and the rain. The one who offers the prayer acknowledges our L-rd as the power that causes rain. The prayer also contains petitions for the fertility of the ground and protection from famine.

Near the end of the prayer, the person praying invokes the names of Abraham, Isaac, Jacob, Moses, Aaron, and the twelve tribes of Israel. The prayer says, "For their merit, favor us with abundant rains, for a blessing and not for a curse, for life and not for death, for plenty and not for famine. Amen."

Today prayers are recited in the synagogues during the Amidah, or standing prayer time. There is an Amidah, composed of eighteen separate benedictions, for the morning, afternoon, and evening services.

From this morning service at Shemini Atzeret until the first day of Passover, whenever the prayer for the dew is said, the following sentence is added to every Amidah prayer at the beginning of the second benediction: "Cause the wind to blow and the rain to fall." This insertion is referred to as the insertion for "the power of our L-rd." Traditional Judaism asks the one who causes the wind to blow and the rain to fall, to show them favor because of the Patriarchs.

At one time the entire nation of Israel celebrated Shemini Atzeret in the natural sense. In our day there is virtually no understanding or celebration of this holiday in rabbinic Judaism. The rabbis have inserted another one of their man-made holidays in its place.

As Messianic believers, we do not ask the L-rd our G-d to show us favor because of the Patriarchs, because we know that they were sinners just as we are sinners. None of their acts of righteousness was ever sufficient to pay for their sin and ensure them entrance into the Eternal Kingdom. We urge unbelievers to repent and believe on Yeshua the Messiah. Only His sacrifice is acceptable for entrance into the Eternal Kingdom. Whenever anyone repents and believes on Yeshua the Messiah, he becomes one with Him, is seated spiritually in heavenly realms (Ephesians 2), becomes a new creation, and has her sin taken away by His righteousness. He is the fountain of true living water. Whoever comes to Him will never thirst again. We tell all who will listen to follow the one about whom Moses wrote in Deuteronomy 18:15ff: "the L-rd will raise up for you a prophet like me from among your own brothers. You must listen to

Him."

The Apostle Paul repeated the same admonition in Acts 26:22 when he spoke before Festus. He said, "But I have had our G-d's help to this very day, and so I stand here and testify to small and great alike. I am saying nothing beyond what the prophets and Moses said would happen. Messiah would suffer and, as the first to rise from the dead, would proclaim light to His own people and to the Gentiles."

We proclaim the words from Matthew 3:17 to all who will listen. A voice spoke from heaven, saying, "'This is my Son whom I love; with Him I am well pleased.'" Seek Him for eternal life in Heaven. If you do not, the Scriptures tell us that you will spend eternity in the Lake of Fire.

In the spiritual sense, there were always people in the nation of Israel who were part of the new creation; they loved the L-rd their G-d with all their hearts, souls and minds. They were obedient to His statutes and precepts and waited in Paradise for Messiah to come to bring them into the Eternal Kingdom. In the times of the New Covenant to Israel, in which we live today, our Father is constantly drawing both Jews and Gentiles unto Himself to be the bride of his Son, Yeshua-Jesus the Messiah.

Asher Levy was a man who looked for God's own heart. He was born in Yugoslavia, raised in an Orthodox home, and became an Orthodox Jewish rabbi for thirty-five years. When he was still quite young, he was taught to say his formal prayers and to wear his phylacteries as prescribed in Deuteronomy 6:8 and 11:18.

At the age of fifteen he went to the theological school for rabbis. While he was there, he studied the Holy Scriptures (Old Testament) and the Talmudic commentaries. Six years later he was ordained as a rabbi in Romania. Afterwards he served in Belgium, England, and California.

Outwardly, he was happy and successful in his ministry, while inwardly he was restless and discontented. He suffered because of the emptiness of life in general. After much turmoil he met a Jewish man with whom he discussed the matter. He did not know it then, but this man was a believer in Messiah Jesus. The advice he gave Levy was to read Isaiah 53.

He proceeded to read this well-known chapter concerning Jesus of Nazareth, which says that He was wounded for our transgressions and bruised for our iniquities. After reading this, Asher Levy felt a great urge to devote time for further study of this subject in the Hebrew Scriptures. He found these words written by the same prophet: "For to us a child is born, to us a son is given and the government will be on his shoulders. And he will be called Wonderful Counselor, Mighty God, Everlasting Father, Prince of Peace. Of the increase of His government and peace there will be no end. He will reign on David's throne and over his kingdom, establishing and upholding it with justice and righteousness that time on and forever. The zeal of the L-RD Almighty will accomplish this" (Is. 9:6-7).

He also read, "Hear now, you house of David! Is it not enough to try the patience of men? Will you try the patience of my G-d also? Therefore the L-RD himself will give you a sign: The virgin will be with child and will give birth to a son, and will call him Immanuel" (Is. 7:13, 14). Immanuel means "G-d with us."

These Scriptures proved to him that Jesus was and is the Messiah in whom all the prophecies were fulfilled. Meanwhile, he had found a clear portrait of the Messiah in a small book that someone had given him. It was his first introduction to the New Testament Scriptures.

He started reading it, like any other book, from the beginning: "The book of the generation of Jesus Christ, the Son of David, the son of Abraham," and found to his amazement that he was reading a Jewish book about a Jew. By reading it carefully, he concluded that Jesus Christ was a Jew of the race of Abraham and David and that He was born of a Jewish virgin of a Jewish tribe, the tribe of Judah, in the Jewish town of Bethlehem.

Because he knew the Law and the Prophets, he followed the record of Messiah on His journeys through the Holy Land, listened to "His beautiful sayings and teachings and observed and admired His compassion and healings." It became his spiritual food. Messiah's promise of forgiveness of sins and eternal life to those who believe in Him drew him until he trusted Jesus as his Messiah and his personal Savior. In his memoirs Levy says "I want to confirm the fact that my heart does not condemn me for my new belief, because I feel that I am still a Jew and shall always be a Jew. I have not renounced our inheritance of Abraham, Isaac, and Jacob. Like Paul, I can say after my acceptance of Christ as my Savior, 'Are they Hebrews? So am I. Are they Israelites? So am I. Are they the seed of Abraham? So am I'" (2 Cor. 11:22).

He repeated with pride the word of Romans 1:16, "For I am not ashamed of the gospel of Christ; for it is the power of God unto salvation to every one that believeth; to the Jew first and also to the Greek" (KJV).

The brilliant example of the great Apostle Paul influenced him very much and gave him the courage to accept the Lord Jesus as his personal Savior. At the beginning Paul was a zealous persecutor of Christ and then became his most faithful follower. Paul was a disciple of that great doctor of the Law, Raban (Rabbi) Gamaliel, at whose feet he sat. It is believed that Raban Gamaliel became a follower of Christ before Paul did.

The basis for this belief comes from the passage of Scripture that records that the Sanhedrin wanted to kill Peter and the other Apostles because they were preaching Christ so boldly. "But a Pharisee named Gamaliel, a teacher of the law, who was honored by all the people, stood up in the Sanhedrin and ordered that the men be put outside for a little while. Then he addressed them: 'Men of Israel, consider carefully what you intend to do to these men . . . I advise you: Leave these men alone! Let them go! For if their purpose or activity is of human origin, it will fail. But if it is from our G-d, you will not be able to stop these men; you will find only yourselves fighting against our G-d" (Acts 5:34, 35, 38, 39).

It has been two thousand years since the Galilean, Yeshua- Jesus, traversed the hills and dales of Israel; and still He is master of the world. His gospel is still preached, and Christ's name as Messiah of Israel is still proclaimed. His message is still repeated everywhere: "For G-d so loved the world, that He gave His only begotten Son, that whosoever believeth In Him should not perish but have everlasting life" (John 3:16 [KJV]).

What are the implications of Shemini Atzeret under the New Covenant?

On Shemini Atzeret, the sacrifices consisted of one bull, one ram, seven perfect male lambs, and one male goat. This is the same basic sacrifice for the Feast of Trumpets and the Day of Atonement (Num. 29:2-5,

Shemini Atzeret: The Eighth Assembly

8, 11). Sukkot, with its multiple sevens, denoted that all sacrificing would be complete one day in the future. Shemini Atzeret, the eighth convocation, is actuality the start of something completely new. It is the start of the new creation after the existing old creation was completed. The new creation is the new spiritual creation in Messiah Yeshua.

Under the Old Covenant there are three classes of people that must receive forgiveness for their sin, with a corresponding sacrifice for each.

A bull is sacrificed for the sins of the High Priest as leader of the priesthood (Lev. 4:3).

A bull also is sacrificed for the sins of the whole congregation (Lev. 4:14).

The sacrifice for forgiveness of sin of the ruling class is a male goat without defect (Lev. 4:23).

The ram is a guilt-offering sacrifice for someone who has defrauded another. The entire congregation of Israel (every single individual from top to bottom) had defrauded Jehovah Elohim at one time or another by the hypocrisy of its attitudes or actions.

The seven lambs signified completion of the sacrifice. Year after year the sacrificial system continued, while the promise of the new creation with its forgiveness of all sins never came to fruition. Then, in the fullness of time, everything came together in just one year. Messiah was sacrificed at Passover, the just for the unjust. He spent time in the lower part of the earth and rose on the third day to sit at the right hand of His father in Heaven.

At the Feast of Weeks, His spirit came down and indwelt many thousands of Jewish people with the knowledge that Yeshua was the long-awaited Messiah. On the Day of Atonement in the same year, our Father's glory left the Temple and He no longer forgave Israel for her sins.

Sukkot, with its many cycles of seven, completed the old creation. Shemini Atzeret was the symbol of the new creation in Messiah Jesus. The Scripture tells us "in Christ . . . the old has gone, the new has come" (2 Cor. 5:17). In this creation, Messiah Jesus paid for all the sins of

160 Shemini Atzeret: The Eighth Assembly

all the people who would come to Him. He paid for the sins of the spiritual leaders of different religions; he paid for the sins of all rulers of the countries of the world who would come to Him; and He paid for all the sins of all the individual people of all time who would come to Him. He is the only acceptable sacrifice for all classes of people, the great Savior and the last hope for all humanity.

The sacrificial process for personal and corporate sin, as well as trespass, is now complete in Yeshua, Jesus the Messiah. Generation after generation of the people of Israel, as well as those of the nations, looked for a Savior who would give eternal peace. Generation after generation of the people of Israel looked for the Messiah, and generation after generation of Gentiles looked for someone to give them salvation and peace.

Israel's eyes were clouded, and she could not see the connection between the Feast of Trumpets, the Day of Atonement, the Feast of Tabernacles, and Shemini Atzeret.

The Feast of Trumpets announced that something miraculous was going to happen. The Day of Atonement announced forgiveness of all sin; the Feast of Tabernacles announced that the current creation was closed; and Shemini Atzeret, the eighth convocation, announced that all sacrifice was now complete. This was a new day and a new dawning.

In Messiah, our Father, made the only sacrifice that would suffice for repentant sinners to be forgiven for all their sin. The only requirement Messiah Jesus made was that they must come to Him to receive that forgiveness. He was only one sacrifice, but that sacrifice was sufficient. He paid for all the sins of all the people of all time that our Father would draw unto Himself. These drawn people, because they have had their sins paid for by Yeshua and are indwelt by the Holy Spirit, have become new creations.

While they eat physical food, their true food is spiritual food that comes from heaven above. Because they are new creations, their wills are not their own; but they are gradually being changed to conform to the will of their Heavenly Father.

In John 7:37 ff. we read about something that happened on the Feast of Tabernacles in the year before Messiah was sacrificed. "On the last and greatest day of the Feast, Jesus (Yeshua) stood and said in a loud

Shemini Atzeret: The Eighth Assembly 161

voice, 'If anyone is thirsty, let him come to me and drink. Whoever believes in me, as the Scripture has said, streams of living water will flow from within him.' By this He meant the Spirit whom those who believed in Him were later to receive. Up to that time the Spirit had not been given, since Jesus (Yeshua) had not yet been glorified." Messiah was welcoming everyone to partake of the new creation that would start on Shemini Atzeret of the following year.

The Lord Yeshua bids everyone come. We announce to everyone who will listen: "This may be the day of your salvation. Do not let salvation pass by you. Believe on the Lord Yeshua the Messiah and you will be saved." Yeshua invited the entire congregation of Israel to come and drink the living water, just as He had previously extended a similar invitation to the woman at the well (John 4).

Water maintains human life and causes crops to grow. It is easy to see how water became a symbol of life in a land as arid as Israel. Yet the invitation was not to those who merely thirst for water, but rather to those who hunger and thirst for righteousness. It was not only to Israel, but it also fulfilled the predictions written about the Gentiles coming to Messiah (Deut.32:43, Ps. 117:1 and Isa.11:10). For what do you hunger and thirst? Is it our Father's righteousness, or is it your own glory?

This invitation was to those whose hearts pant after our Father: "as a deer pants after water" (Ps. 42:1, 2). The water that Yeshua offers satisfies completely. It produces a well of living waters, springing up into everlasting life. That which Messiah presented as a spring to the woman at the well is, in our day, a flowing river (John 4:13-15; 7:38).

The act of drinking refers to believing in Yeshua. "If any man is thirsty, let him come to me and drink" (John 7:37). The invitation is not to the Law of Moses, but to Yeshua alone. To come to Yeshua and drink is to believe on Him alone as Savior and the source of eternal life. The bubbling inner spring and the thundering flow of living water are references to the Holy Spirit and His ministry of indwelling all who believe (John 14:17 and 1 Cor. 12:13).

Yeshua introduced the statement "from his innermost being shall flow rivers of living water." While there is no exact statement like this in the Older Testament, there are numerous Scriptures that link the symbol of water with the outpouring of the Holy Spirit.

The Prophet Isaiah wrote from our Father, "For I will pour out water on the thirsty land, and streams on the dry ground; I will pour out my Spirit on your offspring, and my blessings on your descendants" (Isa. 44:3). Isaiah parallels the thirsty land with the future generations of Israel and links water with the Holy Spirit. The similarity to the words of Yeshua is unmistakable. The idea of living waters was not foreign to Yeshua's listeners.

Zechariah spoke of life-giving Messianic streams, "On that day living water will flow out from Jerusalem, half to the eastern sea and half to the western sea, in summer and in winter" (Zech. 14:8). This is the promise of eternal life with Messiah forever. We could also include Joel 2:23, Zech. 13:1, and a number of other passages that link together or allude to a relationship between water and a pouring out of the Holy Spirit. The majority of these Older Testament passages point to our Father's activity in the end time.

The prophet Ezekiel wrote, "For I will take you out of the nations; I will gather you from all the countries and bring you back into your own land. I will sprinkle clean water on you, and you will be clean; I will cleanse you from all your impurities and from all your idols. I will give you a new heart and put a new spirit in you; I will remove from you your heart of stone and give you a heart of flesh. And I will put my Spirit in you and move you to follow my decrees and be careful to keep my laws" (Ezek. 36:24ff.). Clearly, this is the promise of the New Covenant as outlined in Jeremiah 31:31ff. (Notice who is going to do the work. Our Father is the doer and we are the recipients.)

The prophet combined thoughts of living water, the outpouring of the Spirit, the Messianic times, and the final redemption of the Jewish people. That is why Yeshua assumed that Nicodemus would understand when He said, "'I tell you the truth, no one can enter the kingdom of our G-d unless he is born of water and the Spirit" (John 3:5).

At Shemini Atzeret, Y'shua is saying, "Believe on me and you will have eternal life with me in Heaven. If you do not, you will go to the lake of the everlasting burnings." I ask you now, where will you go? Will it be to Heaven or to the lake of the everlasting burning? Messiah Yeshua

Himself says, "Come unto me. Believe on Me." He says that whosoever will, may come. If you feel personally in your heart that you can't come, ask our Heavenly Father for the strength and the ability to recognize and come to His Son for salvation.

It does not matter what you have done, what you look like, or how old you are. Yeshua invites you to Himself so that you may have eternal life. Yeshua was the perfect sacrifice prepared, not by human hands, but by the hands of our Father Himself, as the only sacrifice acceptable for man's sin (John 19:30).

He was given, not by accident, but by the determinate counsel and foreknowledge of our Almighty Father (Acts 2:23). Yeshua said that it was finished (John 19:30). The it to which He is refers is sacrificing. All sacrificing is finished because He was the final sacrifice.

If you are not a believer in Messiah Yeshua, I bid you to come to Him now. Come to Yeshua, the author and finisher of eternal salvation in Heaven.

The Sabbath

INTRODUCTION

Disagreements over the observance, the non-observance, and the mode of celebrating the Sabbath have become an issue and the cause of much dissension in worship today.. The heart of this conflict lies in differing understandings of the nature, function, and duration of the Sabbath.

Some hold that the Sabbath that was given in the Older Covenant Scriptures is still in effect, and that we should celebrate it on Saturday. Some believe that, since the New Covenant Scriptures do not repeat a command for its observance, the practice of keeping the Sabbath on Saturday is invalid. They maintain that while Saturday is the Jewish Sabbath, Sunday has become the Christian Sabbath. Still others say that the Sabbath, as we know it in the Older Covenant Scriptures, is no longer in effect and that believers should celebrate on Sunday (the original day of the Feast of First Fruits), since that is the day Messiah rose to be with His Father in Heaven. Another group looks for the fulfillment of the Sabbath in Messiah, who is the fulfiller of the Sabbath. They believe that in Messiah Yeshua, there is a New Creation, where the day of worship is neither spelled out nor accentuated.

In actuality, in the New Creation a specific day of worship is not ordained; worship of our Bridegroom and Master is to be continual. It is to occur regardless of what we are doing, for all our waking hours seven days a week. The important point to remember is that Yeshua-Jesus is the Messiah of Israel and the Savior of the nations. He and He alone deserves all worship all the time.

Many worthy saints who have gone before us looked for the time when Israel would recognize Yeshua-Jesus as her true Lord. Charles Hodge, a great theologian of the last century wrote the following:

The second great event, which according to the common faith of the church, which is to precede the second advent of Christ, is the national conversion of the Jews …. that there is to be such a national conversion may be argued ... from the original call and destination of that people. Our L-rd called Abraham and promised that through him, and in his seed, all the nations of the earth should be blessed . A presumptive argument is drawn from the strange preservation of the Jews through so many centuries as a distinct people.

As the rejection of the Jews was not total, so neither is it final. First, the L-rd G-d did not design to cast away His people entirely, but by their rejection, in the first place to facilitate the progress of the Gospel among the Gentiles, and ultimately to make the conversion of the Gentiles the means of converting the Jews ... Because if the rejection of the Jews has been a source of blessing, much more will their restoration be the means of good ... The restoration of the Jews to the privileges of our G-ds people is included in the ancient predictions and promises made respecting them ... The plan of our G-d, therefore, contemplated the calling of the Gentiles, the temporary rejection and final restoration of the Jews .

He shows that the rejection of the Jews was not intended to result in their being finally cast away, but to secure the more rapid progress of the Gospel among the heathen, in order that their conversion might react upon the Jews, and be the means of bringing all, at last, within the fold of the Redeemer.

The future restoration of the Jews is, in itself, a more probable event than the introduction of the Gentiles into the church of our L-rd. This, of course, supposes that our L-rd regarded the Jews, on account of their relation to Him, with peculiar favor, and that there is still something in their relation to the ancient servants of our L-rd and His covenant with them, which causes them to be regarded with special interest. As men look upon the children of their early friends with kinder feelings than on the children of strangers, our L-rd refers to this fact to make us sensible that He still retains purposes of peculiar mercy towards His ancient people.

As the restoration of the Jews is not only a most desirable event, but one which our L-rd has determined to accomplish, Christians should keep it constantly in view even in their labors for the conversion of the Gentiles. (Systematic Theology, V3, James Clark & Co. 1906, p. 805 and A Commentary on the Epistle to the Romans, Presbyterian Board of Publication, 1836, pp. 270-285, passim. Now published by Banner of Truth Trust.)

THREE QUESTIONS AND THEIR ANSWERS

How and why was the Sabbath day established?

How was and is the Sabbath day celebrated?

What are the implications of the Sabbath day under the New Covenant?

How and why was the Sabbath day established?

The premier text on the Sabbath comes from Exodus 20:8-11. "Remember the Sabbath day by keeping it holy. Six days you shall labor and do all your work, but the seventh day is a Sabbath to the L-rd our G-d . On it you shall not do any work, neither you nor your son or daughter, nor your manservant or maidservant, nor your animals, nor the alien within your gates. For in six days the L-rd made the heavens and the earth, the sea, and all that is in them, but He rested on the seventh day. Therefore the L-rd blessed the Sabbath day and made it holy."

The Sabbath commandment is part of the group of commandments we call the Ten Commandments. It cannot be considered independently of the other nine commandments, nor can it be taken independently of the multitude of other injunctions that our L-rd gave to Israel. In total, according to Jewish authority, there are 613 laws of the Torah. Some of the laws were for men; others were for women; and still others concerned temple worship. As a body, these laws defined Israel and her relationship to her L-rd and G-d.

How was and is the Sabbath day celebrated?

Given the multitude of laws and injunctions that our L-rd gave to Israel, it was not possible for anyone except Messiah to be able to accomplish all of the Law's requirements. The purpose of giving Israel the commandments and laws was to show her what she needed for her spiritual salvation. It is a foregone conclusion that she could not possibly complete them; and, therefore, she would not be able to become acceptable to Yahweh Elohim.

Our Sovereign L-rd set Israel apart and gave her the Sabbath so that in her day of rest they would remember Him; she was to call to mind the salvation He gave them from oppression in Egypt and His gift of the land of milk and honey. The Sabbath was to remind her that each of the people was in a personal covenantal relationship with Him as Creator and Savior, and to remind her of her obligation to follow His precepts.

Throughout the Older Covenant Scriptures we find other injunctions regarding the Sabbath. From Exodus 31:13-17 we learn that anyone who desecrates the Sabbath by working must be put to death. Israel, and not the Gentiles, was to observe the Sabbath in her generations as a lasting covenant. Say to the Israelites, "… this will be a sign between me and you for the generations to come [forever]" (Ex. 31:13, emphasis added).

In Ezekiel 20:12 the prophet records the words of our L-rd that were given to him, "Also I gave them my Sabbaths as a sign between us, that they would know that I the L-rd made them holy.'"

Notice that the Scripture is clear in these verses: our L-rd our G-d gave the Sabbath to Israel and not to the Nations. Additionally, it was our L-rd our G-d who would make Israel holy. Anyone who knows and understands the 613 laws of Torah realizes that it was impossible for Israel or any other nation, in and of itself, to complete them.

A summary of the requirements of the Sabbath is as follows:

No one may leave home (Exodus 16:29b).

No one may work (Exodus 20:10).

No one may cook (Exodus 35:3).

Observation of the Sabbath is coupled with the honoring of one's parents (Leviticus 19:3).

Every Sabbath one was to set special bread before the L-rd (Leviticus 24:5-8).

No one may gather wood (Numbers 15:32).

On the Sabbath day, one was to make double the animal sacrifices as well as the meat and drink offerings (Numbers 28:1-10).

Visits may be made to men of G-d (2 Kings 4:23).

No one may carry a burden (Jeremiah 17:21).

No one may buy or sell (Amos 8:5).

The Sabbath was restrictive because our L-rd, wanted the children of Israel to be free from the distractions of this world when they were to have communion with Him.

In Leviticus 11:45, our Father reminds the Israelites why they are to follow His commandments. "I am the L-rd who brought you up out of Egypt, to be your G-d; therefore be holy, because I am holy." Holiness as defined in the Holy Scriptures can come only from our L-rd . As Israel would attempt to follow His statutes from their hearts, He would make them holy. Deuteronomy 6:25 says, "… if we are careful to obey all this law before the L-rd our G-d, as He has commanded us, that will be our righteousness" (emphasis added). Human beings have no righteousness in and of themselves; their righteousness can come only from doing all of our L-rd's commandments. The giving of the Sabbath was to establish a personal commitment between each member of the nation of Israel and his Sovereign Lord. If a person did all the law, he had righteousness; if a person did not do all the law, he did not have any righteousness.

The Sabbath, in the times of the Older Covenant, was the hinge pin that would enable the children of Israel to complete the balance of the Ten Commandments and all of our L-rd's statutes in His own righteousness. The individual would complete and fulfill the law when he threw himself upon Yahweh for mercy, because only then could he keep the totality of the law. By keeping the Sabbath day holy and not just refraining from work, people would create an atmosphere in their homes that would fulfill the Sovereign King's first three commandments and give them His strength to uphold all the other statutes that he had given them.

After reviewing the commandments in the beginning of Deuteronomy 5 we see that the chapter ends with these words from verse 32, "So be careful to do what your L-rd your G-d has commanded you; do not turn aside to the right or to the left. Walk in all the way that your L-rd your G-d has commanded you, so that you may live and prosper and prolong your days in the land that you will possess."

In Deuteronomy 6, Moses begins his recitation of the commands, decrees, and laws that the L-rd his G-d told him to teach Israel. We read that his L-rd and his G-d promises the blessing of a good life in a good land if the people will fear Him and follow His decrees. "Hear O Israel: the L-rd your G-d is one. Love the L-rd your G-d with all your heart and all your soul and all your strength. These commandments that I give you this day are to be upon your hearts. Impress them on your children. Talk about them when you sit at home and when you walk along the road, when you lie down and when you get up. Tie them as symbols on your hands and bind them on your foreheads. Write them on the door frames of your houses and on your gates." (Vs. 4-9) the L-rd our G-d gave Israel His Sabbath so that the individual Israelites would stop their daily routine and seek Him for strength and wisdom to be able to fulfill His commandments, decrees, and statutes.

How was and is the Sabbath Day celebrated?

Israel as a nation was just like any other people. She was of the natural creation and sought the things that she could taste, touch, and smell. Within that natural creation there was always a remnant that strove after the Lord and sought to fulfill His regulations from their hearts. They understood the Scriptures that say, "The fear of the L-rd is the beginning of wisdom; the fear of the L-rd is the beginning of knowledge" (Ps. 111:10a; Prov. 1:7a). Those of the remnant remembered how their Sovereign King had dealt with the Egyptians and with the nations whose land He had given them. They had a healthy fear of what He could do and they loved Him even more because of what He had done.

Time after time the Lord Almighty chastised Israel as a nation for her Sabbath violations. By violating the Sabbath, she was dishonoring her L-rd and His word. After a period of time, her Sovereign L-rd sent her into captivity for seventy years so the land would receive the Sabbath rests that were due it.

There were also periods of great revival when it was evident that the spirit of the L-rd was stirring the people to be observant to the will and laws of their G-d. Just as there were many homes in the past, many homes today revere the Sabbath day and keep it holy. The Sabbath day not only was for rest and separation from the world's activities, but it also was for the contemplation and adoration of the L-rd our G-d for His faithfulness.

To understand Israel's view of the Sabbath, we must consider it in light of the rest of the laws of our L-rd our G-d. Within the five books of Moses we have the famous 613 laws of the Torah that many people talk about and few know and understand: some are for men; some are for women; and some deal with religious worship. Within the 613 laws, our Sovereign King gave Israel Ten Commandments. Within those ten the first three deal specifically with Israel's relationship to her Sovereign. By observing the fourth commandment in the way our L-rd wanted her to observe it, she would be given strength and energy to draw closer to Him personally.

This closeness would engender within the people; a love to do His will. But, alas, even though Israel was set apart as a separate people and given laws and precepts to follow as a nation, she chose not to follow our Father's ways. Instead, she followed the evil ways of the countries around her.

In the time of the prophet Jeremiah Yahweh in His grace and mercy once again gave the people a chance to repent of their evil and turn from their evil ways. They chose to reject their L-rd's pleadings and, instead, followed the desires of their hearts. Their L-rd then sent them into captivity in Babylon. During their captivity, some groups promoted the Sabbath day so that the Israelites would remain separate and not become absorbed into the Babylonian culture.

Eventually, the Pharisees emerged as a distinct religious and political group that fostered personal responsibility and strict observance of the Sabbath. They maintained that, in addition to the written law, there was also an Oral Law given to Moses at Sinai. This law was not written, but was passed orally by holy men from generation to generation. They maintained that all of Israel was to observe this oral law in addition to the written Law in Torah. They worked closely with the people, encouraging them toward holiness.

The Pharisees were jealous of the power of the Temple priests and sought to undermine their authority whenever they could. They developed synagogues to promote their theology among the people on a weekly basis. The average Israelite would come to Jerusalem to worship at the Temple only three times a year for the Levitical convocations. He felt removed from the priesthood. The people felt closer to the Pharisees, since they attended synagogues weekly for the teaching and preaching services held there.

As a result of weekly synagogue meetings, the Sabbath day observance eventually changed from personal individual observance to one of corporate worship on a weekly basis. The L-rd our G-d in His written word, never told the Pharisees or anyone else to do this. There is no place in Scripture that our L-rd commands corporate worship on a specific day, nor does He instruct people to have corporate worship one or more times a week. The Judeo-Christian culture worships weekly without any written revelation, because the Pharisees started that process and the apostles continued it.

The Pharisees rejected the idea that the L-rd was only in the Temple. They believed that He was everywhere and, therefore, believed that their Synagogue worship would be as equally pleasing to Him as the Temple worship.

After the destruction of the Temple, the people were forced to look to the teachings of the Pharisees as a guide for their daily life as well as for instruction on how they could enter into the eternal kingdom. Their formula for attaining eternal life in Heaven came to be called Rabbinic Judaism. Both the Ultra Orthodox and Orthodox communities practice a Pharisaic form of Rabbinic Judaism. In the Orthodox and Ultra Orthodox communities the Sabbath is rigorously observed and becomes part of their system of works that will give the people entrance into the eternal kingdom. Other branches of Judaism practice their own versions of Rabbinic Judaism, which vary from the conservative to the ultra-liberal.

Many Jewish people today treat the Sabbath with honor and reverence. They look forward to the coming of the Sabbath so that they can take their rest in the L-rd. Within these groups the Sabbath is held in higher regard than any other holiday. It is a family day when parents and children do things together at home or in the synagogue.

In the Orthodox and Ultra Orthodox systems of Rabbinic Judaism there is a special list of activities that are prohibited on the Sabbath, because it is a time when everyone should focus on the L-rd our G-d and not on the pressures of the world around them. Generally, the following regulations are in force now: no buying, selling, or doing any other work; no cooking or purchasing of food or any other supplies; no carrying of burdens for any appreciable distance; and walking only for a limited specified distance (usually to a synagogue service). Because cooking is prohibited on the Sabbath, there is a festive meal before the Sabbath begins on Friday. This is the time when the father will bless his wife as well as their children. During the day on Saturday everyone eats food that was cooked before sundown on Friday.

On Saturday after sundown a special meal is prepared again. It is a joyful time when anyone who observes the Sabbath feels a direct connection with all other people who are also celebrating this convocation. The meal on Friday night welcomes in the Sabbath, while the meal on Saturday night bids it goodbye for another week.

In addition to Jewish people, varied groups of Christians celebrate the Sabbath and worship on Saturdays. Generally speaking, while they worship on Saturday, they do not follow the restrictions of either Biblical or Rabbinic Judaism.

What are the Implications of the Sabbath day under the New Covenant?

While the New Covenant Scriptures do not say that people ought to worship on the Sabbath day (Saturday), it is also true that they do not say that people are not to worship on the Sabbath day. The exact same statement can be said for Sunday worship. Messiah Yeshua- Jesus went to the synagogues to speak to people on the Sabbath because that is where they congregated and because He was sent to the lost sheep of the house of Israel (Matthew 15:24). The Apostle Paul, who wrote that the gospel was to go to the Jew first and then go to the Greek, also went into the synagogues on Saturday to speak with the Jewish people.

There is no Scriptural injunction in the New Covenant telling born again believers when they must have their corporate worship. There's also no Scriptural injunction in the New Covenant telling the children of God how their service is to be conducted.

It is a significant note that the Sabbath is the only convocation that is given the importance of being mentioned in the Decalogue. The Sabbath rest was given only to Israel. The Scriptures tell us of many godly men who lived before the Decalogue was given to Israel, and none of them were instructed to observe the Sabbath. The Sabbath was not given to the nations, but only to Israel. It was not even given to Abraham as the father of the Jewish nation. If it had been given to Abraham, then believers after the crucifixion of Messiah could possibly claim that the Sabbath should be legally followed as the day of worship without any of the legal requirements because they are spiritual seed of Abraham. But it was not given to Abraham or Isaac but only as a law and commandment to the children of Jacob.

Messiah Yeshua- Jesus said that He is Lord of the Sabbath day (Matthew 12:8, Mark 2:28, and Luke 6:5). For believers, Messiah Jesus is their Sabbath rest as well as their spiritual Sabbath food. Messiah Yeshua and Messiah Yeshua alone is their burden bearer, their salvation, their Savior, their Lord, their bridegroom, and their peace. There is now no condemnation in them: they are in Messiah. They walk not after the flesh but after the Spirit (Romans 8:1). They have not received the spirit of bondage to fear, but they have received the spirit of adoption whereby they cry "Abba, Father," The Spirit of our Father is a witness with their spirit that they are His children. They are the heirs of our G-d and joint heirs with Messiah. We suffer with Him so that we may also be glorified with Him (Romans 8:15-17).

As believers we are a "new creation, old things have passed away behold all things have become new" (II Corinthians 5:17). Those who are reborn by the Spirit of the living God are strangers and sojourners in this world. They are the spiritual descendants of Abraham who looked for a city that had foundations whose builder and maker was G-d (Hebrews 11:10.

The true home for these believers is in the heavenly realms, the abode of the L-rd G-d the Creator and Sustainer of all things. A believer has been raised up in the spirit and now sits with Messiah in the heavenly realms. In the ages to come the Father will show great riches of His grace toward us through Messiah Jesus (Ephesians 2:6-7).

Our Sabbath rest is not a day; it is, firstly, a person and, secondly, a place. Our Sabbath rest is in Messiah Yeshua, the One whose kingdom is not of this world. He was a King in His own kingdom and then was born King of this earth and came to be a witness of the truth in this world. Everyone that is of the truth hears His voice (John 18:36-37). Believers in Messiah Yeshua have no part or lot in an earthly Sabbath that is celebrated one day in seven. In reality, all believers are in their Sabbath rest; and they are to celebrate the Sabbath every waking hour, seven days a week. What was celebrated at one time as a special day, to separate a specific people from the world and its entanglements, is now to be celebrated all day everyday that we are still upon this earth.

Our example to the world around us is our detachment from what it considers to be reality and our attachment to what it thinks is foolish. All Believers in the salvation that Messiah Jesus freely gives to all who will come to Him are in direct opposition to the natural world's system of existence. Generally speaking, the natural world believes in what it can see, taste, touch, and smell.

Those who live by the Sprit of Y'shua-Jesus live through His Spirit and consider the only reality to be what they cannot see, what they cannot taste, what they cannot touch, and what they cannot smell (Romans 4:17). Born again believers have washed their wedding garments in the blood of the Lamb who is Messiah Jesus.

Except for very rare cases and in the European Common market, when a person leaves his own country, he must have a passport to enter another country. A believer's passport to the eternal kingdom in heaven is the blood and righteousness of Yeshua, who is L-rd Messiah and Savior. He is King of the place the believer will one day enter to become His bride. A place has already been prepared for him, and in the Spirit he is already there (Ephesians 2:6).

This kingdom accepts only properly validated passports, and the passports are validated only by Yeshua the Righteous. Bearing the blood and righteousness of the L-rd Messiah while we are on this earth is both our Sabbath rest and the celebration of our Sabbath rest. In Ezekiel 20:12 the Sovereign King says that He gave Israel His Sabbaths as a sign between them so that Israel would know that the Sovereign King made her holy (sanctified her). If Israel as a nation had observed the Sabbaths and the Sabbath regulations, the Sovereign King would have made her holy and a kingdom of priests. (While a remnant did observe the Sabbaths, the majority of the nation covering the period of the Older Covenant Scriptures did not.)

In Matthew 5:17 Messiah Yeshua-Jesus says "Do not think that I have come to abolish the law or the prophets; I have not come to abolish them but to fulfill them." Again, Messiah and Messiah only is fulfillment; there is none other.

Let us make it clearer. Messiah Yeshua- Jesus is the total and complete embodiment of all the laws and all the predictions and encouragements of the prophets in the Older Covenant Scriptures. Let us repeat just one more time, "He is the word who was made flesh to come and dwell among us (John 1:14).

When a born again believer is in Messiah Yeshua, he has fulfilled all the law and the prophets, not in himself but in Him, Yeshua. Messiah Yeshua is the total embodiment of the Sabbath; and if we are in Him, we are perpetually in our Sabbath. In John 15 Messiah says that apart from Him believers can do nothing in and of themselves. The Father has loved Him and He loves believers. If believers keep His commandments, they will abide in His love just as He has kept His Father's commands and abides in His Father's love.

The command of Messiah is that believers are to love each other just as He loves them. Believers are His friends if they do what He commands. Believers did not choose Messiah, but He chose believers and appointed them to go and bear fruit that will last (John15:16). 1 John 2:6 tells us that whoever claims to abide in Messiah must walk as He walked. 1 John 2:10 tells us that whoever loves his brother abides in the light.

Verse 17 tells us that the world and its desires pass away, but the man who does the will of his Creator abides forever. True believers will receive eternal life because that anointing abides in them. His anointing is real; and, therefore, believers are taught to abide in Him and do what is right. The effect of the Sabbath on a born again believer's life it that he is totally transformed by the Master of the Sabbath; and He abides in him while he is on this earth, because He is his Sabbath rest. The believer has the peace that passes all understanding, because the Comforter who is called the Holy Spirit and who was sent by Messiah dwells in him for the glory of the Master of the Sabbath, Yeshua the Messiah.

The New Covenant Scriptures in Romans 14 and Colossians 2 teach us how we should live with one another concerning things we may differ about, which includes the Sabbaths. Romans 14:5 says "One Man considers one day more scared than another; another man considers every day alike. Each one should be fully convinced in his own mind." Colossians 2:16 says "Therefore do not let anyone judge you by what you eat or drink, or with regard to a religious Festival a New Moon celebration or Sabbath Day these are a Shadow of things that were to come. The reality however is found in [Messiah Yeshua]." We can safely say that Messiah Yeshua is the reality of the religious festivals, New Moon celebrations, and the Sabbath Day.

To those who say the Sabbath is still in effect and must be celebrated on Saturday, I would say the following: "If you wish to take the Sabbath regulation literally, then you must adhere to all the restrictions that come with it. The answer to question 2 given earlier in this chapter, lists those."

If you say it is a legal requirement to observe the Sabbath day, I would say to you that you have no Biblical, legal, moral, or ethical warrant to take only part of our Creator's 613 laws of the Torah while negating its full ramifications and obligations. You cannot say, "I will celebrate only part of it, because I am in a different dispensation now." In other words you cannot take what you consider to be the best and leave the rest. The Almighty Creator does not say that some of His laws can be observed while others do not have to be. They are either all fulfilled in Messiah, or they are not. There is no middle ground possible. If our Creator Himself does not separate His laws as far as observance is concerned, neither does man have the right to separate the laws he likes and wants to do, form those he does not like and cannot do.

A clear example would be the fact that there is no longer a Temple; therefore, some of the 613 laws cannot be observed because the Temple does not exist. The fact is, the Temple was destroyed because Messiah Yeshua was the end of all sacrificing. There was no longer any need for the Temple sacrificing to cover man's sin when Messiah by His own sacrifice took away the sin of all who would come to Him.

The Father does all things by the counsel of His own will, and that includes destroying a sacrificial system that He and He alone created (Ephesians 1:11).

CONCLUSION

It is not a legal requirement to celebrate the Sabbath on Saturday or any other day. In light of the Romans 14 and Colossians 2 passages, you may worship the L-rd our G-d in a corporate way on any day you want. If you wish to worship on Saturday, for whatever reason, the Scriptures will back you up just as long as you do not impose you belief on someone else or say that someone else who does not observe that day is not as good a believer as you are or does not satisfy our Creator as well as you do.

If you are one who says the Sabbath is still in effect and has been changed to be a Christian Sabbath and has moved from Saturday to Sunday and that we must worship on Sunday, I would say to you the following, "There are no instructions in the New Covenant Scriptures that instruct us to make that change." I would also say to you that the Sabbath rest is not a specific day; it is a specific Person and place. Romans 14 and Colossians 2 would contradict your theory.

If however, you wish to worship on Sunday, and say it is the Christian Sabbath, and even take upon yourself all the restrictions for the Sabbath that Israel had, (even though it is impossible to accomplish), that is your right and prerogative. If you do choose that position for yourself, you are saying in effect that Messiah's work on the cross was insufficient and that you will choose your own righteousness rather than accept our Creators free grace.

If you want to worship the L-rd our G-d who is our Creator and the Sustainer on the old Sabbath, namely Saturday, because that is when our Creator rested after creating the heavens and earth, or for any other reason whatsoever, blessings to you. If you want to worship our Creator on Sunday because that is when the Messiah rose on the Feast of First Fruits to be with His Father, or for any other reason, blessings to you. But do not think other believers have to agree with your position; and, further, do not think that they are disobedient, less observant, inferior believers, or something else, if they do not.

In closing, Messiah is both our Sabbath peace and our Sabbath rest. The restrictions that were put on Israel's observance of the Sabbath in the natural creation have no bearing upon believers who worship in the spiritual creation. While believers should be worshipping the Master of the Sabbath on a continual individual basis, we may also have corporate worship whenever and wherever we desire. Our worship of Him is to be a continual experience, not just one day out of seven. Messiah Yeshua has completely fulfilled the Sabbath Day and all its regulations. Let each person be assured in his own mind.

Below I have included a testimony written by Rabbi Dr. Max Wertheimer.

Rabbi Dr. Max Wertheimer was born in Germany of Orthodox parents in the early part of the twentieth century. The first fifteen years of his life were saturated with training in Orthodox Judaism. He studied the Talmud and the Torah as well as the commentaries of noted Jewish scholars. Although he continued to read the daily prayers and attend the Synagogue regularly, his worldly friends and acquaintances led him into the sinful pleasures of the world around him. His parents were upset and sent him to the Hebrew Union College in the U.S. to continue his studies. There were major cultural differences between the two countries, but he made adjustments and finished his eight years of training in only seven years.

After he became a believer he looked back on that period of his life and made some insightful comments. He says, "My religious views were fostered by tradition, pride, and prejudice. I thought Judaism was the greatest religion as well as the most rational. I believed the theory of evolution, had modernistic notions of free thought, held some socialistic doctrines, and thought that Moses the prophet excelled in genius and perfection and that there was no one equal to him. I loved to go to the theater, attend symphony concerts, read fiction as well as worldly literature, and play my violin. I was swayed by the lust of the eyes, the lust of the flesh, and the pride of life."

Rabbi Wertheimer was diligent in his study of all Jewish religious literature as homiletics and hermeneutics according to rabbinical principles. He was completely proficient in the translation of Hebrew into English and had a full knowledge of Jewish history.

He was ordained and became Rabbi of his first synagogue, where he served for ten years. He contributed much to their knowledge of social, industrial, and economic problems of the day and received many tokens of affection from his flock. He spoke on monotheism, ethical culture, and the moral systems of the Jewish people. He looked forward to Sabbath mornings when he gave addresses on the Pentateuch; on Sundays he taught from eight in the morning to five in the evening with only an hour's break for his mid-day meal.

He became popular as a public speaker and was often asked to speak in Christian churches. He recalled quite vividly the day he proudly stood before an audience of professing Christians and told them why he was a Jew and why he would not believe in their Christ as his Messiah and Savior. He gloried in Reform Judaism that acknowledged no need of an atoning sacrifice for sin. It was religion of ethics which quieted qualms of conscience through smug self-righteousness.

In that audience sat a humble, elderly woman who prayed, "Oh God, bring Dr. Wertheimer to realize his utter need of that Savior he so boastingly rejects! Bring him, if necessary, to the very depths in order that he may know his need of my Lord Jesus Christ." In his musings, Dr Wertheimer said to himself, "Why do I need Jesus? I am perfectly satisfied with my life. My wife is young, attractive, and accomplished. I am Rabbi of the B'nai Yeshorum Synagogue. I live in a beautiful home, enjoy a place of prominence in the community where I live, and have spoken in every denominational church in my area. I was elected an honorary member of the Ministerial Association, served as chaplain in the Masonic Lodge, and fared sumptuously every day."

Suddenly there came a change. His wife became seriously ill and died. He became a distraught widower with two small children. He could not sleep, and He walked the streets striving to find something that would make him forget the void in his life. His dreams were shattered and he could not find comfort. He called on the God of his father, but the heavens seemed as brass. How could he speak words of comfort to others when his own sorrow had brought him to despair?

He delved into Spiritism, Theosophy, and Christian Science only to find them futile and hopeless. He decided that he must resign as Rabbi and take time to think things through. He was perplexed about one thing in particular: "where was the spirit and soul of my loved one who had made my existence so sweet? What had become of all her faculties, the intents and purposes of that active mind?" He turned to the Bible for an answer. Again he studied Judaism, but it answered no questions, and it satisfied no craving in his heart. Then he started to read the New Testament, comparing it with the Old. In Isaiah 53 he was perplexed by the expression "my righteous servant." Who was this One who was going to bear the iniquity of Israel? He decided that it could not mean Israel, for the prophet spoke of her as a sinful nation, laden with iniquity. Who was it?

He began to study the context and in Isaiah 50:6 he found, "I gave My back to the smiter." Then he read how the chapter began: "Thus saith Jehovah." He asked himself, "Does God have a back? Did He give it to the smiters?" Then he read, "He gave His cheeks to them that pluck off the hair." He read how He hid not his face "from shame and spitting." He asked himself, "When did Jehovah have these human characteristics? When and why did He suffer these indignities?" He was further perplexed by Psalm 110:1.

In his utter confusion he began to read the prophet Isaiah from the beginning. He was stopped abruptly at 9:6: "For unto us a child is born, unto us a Son is given, and the government shall be upon His shoulder: His name shall be called Wonderful, Counselor, The Mighty God, The Everlasting Father, The Prince of Peace." This was most incomprehensible to him! He was suddenly faced with the doctrine of the Triune Godhead. Now he had to deal with the popular doxology of Judaism. "Shema Yisrael, Adonai Eloheynu, Adonai, Echod." Upon that one word Echod "one" the entire philosophy of Judaism is based.

His Testimony continues in his own word:

I had been taught by the Rabbis that Echod means absolute unity. I began to study that word and found to my amazement it was used of Adam and Eve, who became one. It was used again when the spies returned from Canaan with a cluster of grapes (Eshol Echod). It was used again when the "men of Judah stood up as one man" (Ish Echod). Suddenly I was struck with the error I had believed and proclaimed through my ministry. Echod cannot mean absolute unity, but a composite unity.

Next I began to search for the name of Jesus in the Old Testament. In my study I found that 275 years before Christ, King Ptolemy Philadelphus summoned men from Palestine and commanded them to translate the Hebrew Scriptures into the Greek vernacular. They took the Pentateuch first, and when they came to "Joshua" they translated it the book of "Jesous," Written with circumflex over it, to show that there had been a suppression of the Hebrew that could not be expressed in the Greek.

When Joshua went into Canaan with the other eleven spies, he was called "Yehoshuah" (Jehovah is Savior). That is exactly what the word Jesus means.

I could hold out in unbelief no longer. I was convinced of the truth God in Christ Jesus. I cried, "Lord, I believe that Thou as Jehovah Yesous has made atonement for me. I believe that Jehovah Yesous died for me. I believe that thou has made provision for me.

From henceforth I will publicly confess Yeshuah as my Saviour and Lord. Thus, after months of searching, I was convinced that Jesus was the righteous servant of Jehovah, Jehovah Tsidkenu, "the Lord our righteousness."

While I had served as a Rabbi I yearned to give the bereaved some hope and comfort, but I could not give what I did not possess. Now I could approach those in heartbreaking grief and tragedy and give them the satisfying words of the Lord Jesus, "I am the resurrection and the life; he that believeth in Me, though he were dead, yet shall he live; and whosoever liveth and believeth in Me shall never die."

And again, "Verily, verily I say unto you: He that heareth My Word, and believeth on him that sent Me, hath everlasting life, and shall not come into condemnation, but is passed from death unto life."

There is but one eternal life, and on source of eternal life; that is G-d's Son. What a great and glorious message we, His redeemed ones, are commissioned to deliver today.

Dr. Wertheimer publicly confessed Jesus as his Messiah and Lord on March 30th, 1904, in the Central Baptist Church in Dayton, Ohio. After graduating from the Southern Baptist seminary in Louisville, Kentucky, he was ordained and served as a pastor for five years in Ada, Ohio. After that he became a Pastor Evangelist with the New Covenant Mission in Pittsburgh, Pennsylvania. After spending 2 and one half years with the Mission, he received a call to become a freelance preacher of the Gospel to both Jew and Gentile. He was in great demand continually as a bible teacher.

If this testimony is intriguing to you PLEASE go to our heavenly Father in prayer, and say to him: Dear Father, I do not in any way shape or form want to take any glory away from you. If you have a Son, and He is the Messiah of Israel, please reveal this to me so that I may worship

Him. Further assisitance is available by calling 717-288-3065.

At 6 o clock in the morning on May 27, 1936, there was a gathering of observant Jewish people waiting for the birth of a child from Marc and Ruth Scalyer. I was given the name Lloyd Elias and was circumcised on the eighth day according to the traditions of our people. I was the only male descendent in our generation of children and I had my bar mitzvah when I was 13 years old.

I attended services regularly on Saturdays and the youth group on Sundays and Thursdays. In addition, for a number of years I was president of Exodus AZA, and am a lifetime member of the B'nai Brith youth organization. After my bar mitzvah, my father encouraged me greatly in my prayer time, and told me that I must also formulate my own prayers from my heart to speak with the L-rd G-d personally. I have done that to this very day.

One day when I was in my upper teens walking outside on the Sabbath, a very aged woman came over to me and took both of my hands in hers. She then started to bless me in Hebrew, Yiddish, and English. At that time I did not know what was up but I greatly valued her blessing. Later on the L-rd G-d sent His Spirit to me and I was reborn in His new creation.

In my service to the L-rd our G-d after we moved to Lancaster Pennsylvania, I have been the Messianic Rabbi for Beth Emmanuel Congregation, a Deacon in Paradise Baptist Church, an Elder at the Lancaster Evangelical Free Church and the founding Spiritual Leader of the Seed of Abraham Messianic Congregation for the past 24 Years.

1 Encyclopedia Judaica, 1972 edition, s.v. "Amnon of Mainz."